The Story of Our Country

Every Child Can Read

Jesse Lyman Hurlbut

Alpha Editions

This edition published in 2024

ISBN : 9789362923271

Design and Setting By
Alpha Editions
www.alphaedis.com
Email - info@alphaedis.com

Contents

A TALK WITH THE YOUNG READER
ABOUT THE HISTORY OF OUR
COUNTRY

IF any of the readers of this book should have the chance to take a railroad ride over the vast region of the United States, from the Atlantic to the Pacific Ocean, from the Great Lakes to the Gulf of Mexico, they would see a wonderful display of cities and towns, of factories and farms, and a great multitude of men and women actively at work. They would behold, spread out on every side, one of the busiest and happiest lands the sun shines upon. Here and there, amid the miles on miles of farms, they might see a forest, here and there a wild beast, here and there a red-faced Indian, one of the old people of the land; but these would be almost lost in the rich and prosperous scene.

If our young traveler knew nothing of history he might fancy that it had been always this way, or that it had taken thousands of years for all those cities to be built and these great fields to be cleared and cultivated. Yet if he had been here only three hundred years ago he would have seen a very different sight. He could not then have gone over the country by railroad, for such a thing had never been thought of. He could not have gone by highroad, for there was not a road of any kind in the whole length and breadth of the land. Nowhere in this vast country would he have seen a city or town; nowhere a ploughed field, a farmhouse, or a barn; nowhere a horse, cow, or sheep; nowhere a man with a white or a black face. Instead of great cities he would have seen only clusters of rude huts; instead of fertile farms, only vast reaches of forest; instead of tame cattle, only wild and dangerous beasts; instead of white and black men, only red-skinned savages.

Just think of it! All that we see around us is the work of less than three hundred years! No doubt many of you have read in fairy tales of wonderful things done by the Genii of the East, of palaces built in a night, of cities moved miles away from their sites. But here is a thing as wonderful and at the same time true, a marvel wrought by men instead of magical beings. These great forests have fallen, these great fields have been cleared and planted, these great cities have risen, these myriads of white men have taken the place of the red men of the wild woods, and all within a period not longer than three times the life of the oldest men now living. Is not this as wonderful as the most marvelous fairy tale? And is it not better to read the true tale of how this was done than stories of the work of fairies and magicians? Let us forget the Genii of the East; men are the Genii of the

West, and the magic of their work is as great as that we read of in the fables of the "Arabian Nights."

The story of this great work is called the "History of the United States." This story you have before you in the book you now hold. You do not need to sit and dream how the wonderful work of building our noble nation was done, for you can read it all here in language simple enough for the youngest of you to understand. Here you are told how white men came over the seas and found beyond the waves a land none of them had ever seen before. You are told how they settled on these shores, cut down the trees and built villages and towns, fought with the red men and drove them back, and made themselves homes in the midst of fertile fields. You are told how others came, how they spread wider and wider over the land, how log houses grew into mansions, and villages into cities, and how at length they fought for and gained their liberty.

Read on and you will learn of more wonderful things still. The history of the past hundred years is a story of magic for our land. In it you will learn of how the steamboat was first made and in time came to be seen on all our rivers and lakes; of how the locomotive was invented and railroads were built, until they are now long enough in our country to go eight times round the earth; of the marvels of the telegraph and telephone—the talking wire; of the machines that rumble and roar in a thousand factories and work away like living things, and of a multitude of marvels which I cannot begin to speak of here.

And you will learn how men kept on coming, and wars were fought, and new land was gained, and bridges were built, and canals were dug, and our people increased and spread until we came to be one of the greatest nations on the earth, and our cities grew until one of them was the largest in the world except the vast city of London. All this and more you may learn from the pages of this book. It is written for the boys and girls of our land, but many of their fathers and mothers may find it pleasant and useful to read.

There are hundreds who do not have time to read large histories, which try to tell all that has taken place. For those this little history will be of great service, in showing them how, from a few half-starved settlers on a wild coast, this great nation has grown up. How men and women have come to it over the seas as to a new Promised Land. How they have ploughed its fields, and gathered its harvests, and mined its iron and gold, and built thousands of workshops, and fed the nations with the food they did not need for themselves.

Year by year it has grown in wealth, until now it is the richest country in the world. Great it is, and greater it will be. But I need say no more. The book has its own story to tell. I only lay this beginning before you as a handy stepping-stone into the history itself. By its aid you may cross the brook and wander on through the broad land which lies before you.

CHAPTER I

COLUMBUS, THE GREAT SAILOR

IF any of my young readers live in Chicago they will remember a wonderful display in that city in 1893. Dozens of great white buildings rose on the shore of the lake, as beautiful as fairy palaces, and filled with the finest of goods of all kinds, which millions of people came to see.

Do you know what this meant? It was what is called a World's Fair, and was in honor of a wonderful event that took place four hundred years before.

Some of you may think that white men have always lived in this country. I hope you do not all think so, for this is not the case. A little more than four hundred years ago no white man had ever seen this country, and none knew that there was such a country on the face of the earth.

It was in the year 1492, that a daring sailor, named Christopher Columbus, crossed a wide ocean and came to this new and wonderful land. Since then men have come here by the millions, and the mighty nation of the United States has grown up with its hundreds of towns and cities. In one of these, which bears the name of Chicago, the grand Columbian World's Fair was held, in honor of the finding of America by the great navigator four hundred years before.

This is what I have set out to tell you about. I am sure you will all be glad to know how this broad and noble land, once the home of the wild red men, was found and made a home for the white people of Europe.

Some of you may have been told that America was really discovered more than four hundred years before Columbus was born. So it was. At that time some of the bold sailors of the northern countries of Europe, who made the stormy ocean their home, and loved the roll of the waves, had come to the frozen island of Iceland. And a ship from Iceland had been driven by the winds to a land in the far west which no man had ever seen before. Was this not America?

Soon after, in the year 1000, one of these Northmen, named Leif Ericson, also known as Leif the Lucky, set sail for this new land. There he found wild grapes growing, and from them he named it Vinland. This in our language would be called Wineland.

After him came others, and there was fighting with the red men, whom they called Skrellings. In the end the Northmen left the country, and before many years all was forgotten about it. Only lately the story has been found again in some old writings. And so time went on for nearly five hundred years more, and nothing was known in Europe about the land beyond the seas.

Now let us go from the north to the south of Europe. Here there is a kingdom called Italy, which runs down into the Mediterranean Sea almost in the shape of a boot. On the western shore of this kingdom is a famous old city named Genoa, in which many daring sailors have dwelt; and here, long ago, lived a man named Columbus, a poor man, who made his living by carding wool.

This poor wool-carder had four children, one of whom (born about 1436) he named Christopher. Almost everybody who has been at school in the world knows the name of this little Italian boy, for he became one of the most famous of men.

Many a boy in our times has to help his father in his shop. The great Benjamin Franklin began work by pouring melted tallow into moulds to make candles. In the same way little Columbus had to comb wool for his father, and very likely he got as tired of wool as Franklin did of candles.

The city he lived in was full of sailors, and no doubt he talked to many of them about life on the wild waters, and heard so many stories of danger and adventure that he took the fancy to go to sea himself.

At any rate we are told that he became a sailor when only fourteen years old, and made long and daring voyages while he was still young. Some of those were in Portuguese ships down the coast of Africa, of which continent very little was known at that time. He went north, too; some think as far as Iceland. Who knows but that he was told there of what the Northmen had done?

Columbus spent some time in the island of Madeira, far out in the Atlantic ocean, and there the people told him of strange things they had seen. These had come over the seas before the west winds and floated on their island shores. Among them were pieces of carved wood, and canes so long that they would hold four quarts of wine between their joints. And the dead bodies of two men had also come ashore, whose skins were the color of bronze or copper.

These stories set Columbus thinking. He was now a man, and had read many books of travel, and had studied all that was then known of geography. For a time he lived by making maps and charts for ship captains. This was in the city of Lisbon, in Portugal, where he married and settled down and had little boys of his own.

At that time some of the most learned people had odd notions about the earth. You may have seen globes as round as an orange, with the countries laid out on them. But the people then had never seen such a globe, and the most of them thought that the earth was as flat as a table, and that any one who sailed too far over the ocean would come to the edge of the earth and fall off.

This seems very absurd, does it not? But you must remember that people then knew very little about the earth they lived on, and could not understand how people could keep on a round globe like flies on a ball of glass.

But there were some who thought the earth to be round, and Columbus was one of these.

At that time silk and spices and other rich goods were brought from China and India, thousands of miles to the east, by caravans that traveled overland. Columbus thought that by sailing west, over the broad Atlantic, he would come to these far countries, just as a fly may walk around the surface of an orange, and come to the place it started from.

The more Columbus thought about this, the more certain he became that he was right. He was so sure of it that he set out to try and make other people think the same way. He wanted ships with which to sail across the unknown seas to the west, but he had no money of his own to buy them with.

Ah! what a task poor Columbus now had. For years and years he wandered about among the kings and princes of Europe, but no one would believe his story, and many laughed at him and mocked him.

First he tried Genoa, the city where he was born, but the people there told him he was a fool or had lost his senses.

Then he went to the king of Portugal. This king was a rascal, and tried to cheat him. He got his plans from him, and sent out a vessel in secret, hoping to get the honor of the discovery for himself. But the captain he sent was a coward and was scared by the rolling waves. He soon came back, and told the king that there was nothing to be found but water and storm. King John, of Portugal, was very sorry afterward that he had tried to rob Columbus of his honor.

Columbus was very angry when he heard what the king had done. He left Portugal for Spain, and tried to get the king and queen of that country to let him have ships and sailors. But they were at war with a people called the Moors, and had no money to spare for anything but fighting and killing.

Columbus stayed there for seven long years. He talked to the wise men, but they made sport of him. "If the earth is round," they said, "and you sail west, your ships will go down hill, and they will have to sail up hill to come back. No ship that was ever made can do that. And you may come to places where the waters boil with the great heat of the sun; and frightful monsters may rise out of the sea and swallow your ships and your men." Even the boys in the street got to laughing at him and mocking him as a man who had lost his wits.

After these many years Columbus got tired of trying in Spain. He now set out for France, to see what the king of that country would do. He sent one of his brothers to England to see its king and ask him for aid.

He was now so poor that he had to travel along the dusty roads on foot, his little son going with him. One day he stopped at a convent called La Rabida, to beg some bread for his son, who was very hungry.

The good monks gave bread to the boy, and while he was eating it the prior of the convent came out and talked with Columbus, asking him his business. Columbus told him his story. He told it so well that the prior believed in it. He asked him to stay there with his son, and said he would write to Isabella, the queen of Spain, whom he knew very well.

So Columbus stayed, and the prior wrote a letter to the queen, and in the end the wandering sailor was sent for to come back to the king's court.

Queen Isabella deserves much of the honor of the discovery of America. The king would not listen to the wandering sailor, but the queen offered to pledge her jewels to raise the money which he needed for ships and sailors.

Columbus had won. After years and years of toil and hunger and disappointment, he was to have ships and sailors and supplies, and to be given a chance to prove whether it was he or the wise men who were the fools.

But such ships as they gave him! Why, you can see far better ones every day, sailing down your rivers. Two of them did not even have decks, but were like open boats. With this small fleet Columbus set sail from Palos, a little port in Spain, on the 3d of August, 1492, on one of the most wonderful voyages that has ever been known.

Away they went far out into the "Sea of Darkness," as the Atlantic ocean was then called. Mile after mile, day after day, on and on they went, seeing nothing but the endless waves, while the wind drove them steadily into the unknown west.

The sailors never expected to see their wives and children again. They were frightened when they started, and every day they grew more scared. They looked with staring eyes for the bleak fogs or the frightful monsters of which they had been told. At one place they came upon great tracts of seaweed, and thought they were in shallow water and would be wrecked on banks of mud. Then the compass, to which they trusted, ceased to point due north and they were more frightened than ever. Soon there was hardly a stout heart in the fleet except that of Columbus.

The time came when the sailors grew half mad with fear. Some of them made a plot to throw Columbus overboard and sail home again. They would tell the people there that he had fallen into the sea and been drowned.

It was a terrible thing to do, was it not? But desperate men will do dreadful things. They thought one man had better die than all of them. Only good fortune saved the life of the great navigator.

One day a glad sailor called his comrades and pointed over the side. A branch of a green bush was floating by with fresh berries on it. It looked as if it had just been broken off a bush. Another day one of them picked from the water a stick which had been carved with a knife. Land birds were seen flying over the ships. Hope came back to their hearts. They were sure now that land must be near.

October 11th came. When night fell dozens of men were on the lookout. Each wanted to be the first to see land. About 10 o'clock that night, Columbus, who was looking out over the waves, saw a light far off. It moved up and down like a lantern carried in a man's hand.

Hope now grew strong. Every eye looked out into the darkness. About two o'clock in the morning came the glad cry of "Land! Land!" A gun was fired from the leading vessel. One of its sailors had seen what looked like land in the moonlight. You may be sure no one slept any more that night.

When daylight came the joyful sailors saw before them a low, green shore, on which the sunlight lay in beauty; men and women stood on it, looking in wonder at the ships, which they thought must be great white-winged birds. They had never seen such things before. We can hardly think what we would have done if we had been in their place.

When the boats from the ships came to the shore, and Columbus landed, clad in shining armor, and bearing the great banner of Spain, the simple natives fell to the ground on their faces. They thought the gods had come from heaven to visit them.

Some of the red-skinned natives wore ornaments of gold. They were asked by signs where they had got this gold, and pointed south. Soon all were on board again, the ships once more spread their sails, and swiftly they flew southward before the wind.

Day by day, as they went on, new islands arose, some small, some large, all green and beautiful. Columbus thought this must be India, which he had set out to find, and he called the people Indians. He never knew that it was a new continent he had discovered.

COLUMBUS AND THE EGG.

The month of March of the next year came before the little fleet sailed again into the port of Palos. The people hailed it with shouts of joy, for they had mourned their friends as dead.

Fast spread the news. When Columbus entered Barcelona, where the king and queen were, bringing with him new plants, birds and animals, strange weapons, golden ornaments, and some of the red-skinned natives, he was received as if he had been a king. He was seated beside the king; he rode by his side in the street; he was made a grandee of Spain; all the honors of the kingdom were showered on him.

We here recall the incident of Columbus and the egg. A dinner was given in his honor and many great men were there. The attention Columbus received made some people jealous. One of them with a sneer asked Columbus if he did not think any one else could have discovered the Indies. In answer Columbus took an egg from a dish on the table and handing it to the questioner asked him to make it stand on end.

After trying several times the man gave it up. Columbus, taking the egg in his hand, tapping it gently on one end against the top of the table so as to break the shell slightly, made it balance.

"Any one could do that," said the man. "So any one can discover the Indies after I have shown him the way," said Columbus.

It was his day of pride and triumph. Poor Columbus was soon to find out how Spain treated those who had given to it the highest honor and the greatest riches. Three times again he sailed to the New World, and once a base Spanish governor sent him back to Spain with chains upon his limbs. Those chains he kept hanging in his room till he died, and asked that they should be buried with him.

They who had once given him every honor, now treated him with shameful neglect. He who had ridden beside the king and dined with the highest nobles of Spain, became poor, sad and lonely.

He died in 1506, fourteen years after his great discovery.

Then Spain, which had treated him so badly, began to honor his memory. But it came too late for poor Columbus, who had been allowed to die almost like a pauper, after he had made Spain the richest country in Europe.

CHAPTER II

THREE GREAT DISCOVERERS

VERY likely some of the readers of this book have asked their fathers or mothers how Spain came to own the islands of Cuba and Porto Rico, whose people they treated so badly that the United States had to go to war a few years ago and take these islands from Spain. Of course, you all know how the battleship *Maine* was blown up in the harbor of the city of Havana, and nearly all its brave sailors went to the bottom and were drowned. That was one reason why we went to war. If you should ask me that question, I would say that these were some of the islands which Columbus found, when he sailed into those sunny seas four centuries ago. They were settled by Spaniards, who killed off all their people and have lived on them ever since. There they have raised sugar cane, and tobacco, and coffee, and also oranges and bananas and all kinds of fine fruits.

They might have kept on owning these islands and raising these fruits for many years to come, if they had not been so cruel to the people that they rose against them, and with the help of the United States Government the islands were taken from Spain.

When Columbus told the nobles and people of Spain of his wonderful discovery, and showed them the plants and animals, the gold and other things, he had found on these far-off islands, it made a great excitement in that country.

You know how the finding of gold in Alaska has sent thousands of our own people to that cold country after the shining yellow metal. In the same way the gold which Columbus brought back sent thousands of Spaniards across the wide seas to the warm and beautiful islands of which the great sailor told them, where they hoped to find gold like stones in our streets.

Dozens of ships soon set sail from Spain, carrying thousands of people to the fair lands of the west, from which they expected to come back laden with riches. At the same time two daring sailors from England, John Cabot and his son Sebastian, crossed the ocean farther north, and found land where the Northmen had found it five hundred years before. In the seas into which the Cabots sailed, great fish were so plentiful that the ships could hardly sail through them, and bears swam out in the water and caught the fish in their mouths. That was certainly a queer way of fishing.

When the Cabots came back and told what they had seen, you may be sure the daring fishermen of Europe did not stay long at home. Soon numbers of their stout little vessels were crossing the ocean, and most of them came back so full of great codfish that the water almost ran over their decks.

Do you not think these fishermen were wiser than the Spaniards, who went everywhere seeking for gold, and finding very little of it? Gold is only good to buy food and other things; but if these can be had without buying they are better still. At any rate, the hardy fishermen thought so, and they were more lucky in finding fish than the Spaniards were in finding gold.

Thus the years passed on, and more and more Spaniards came to the islands of Cuba and Hispaniola (which is now known as Hayti or San Domingo). And some of them soon began to sail farther west in search of new lands. Columbus, in his last voyage, reached the coasts of South America and Central America and other Spanish ships followed to those new shores.

I might tell you many wonderful things about these daring men. One of them was named Balboa, whose story you will be glad to hear, for it is full of strange events. This man had gone to the island of Hispaniola to make his fortune, but he found there only bad fortune. He had to work on a farm, and in time he became so poor and owed so much money that it seemed as if he could never get out of debt. In fact he was in sad straits.

No doubt the people who had lent him money often asked him to pay it back again, and Balboa, who got into a worse state every day, at length took an odd way to rid himself of his troubles. A ship was about to set sail for the west, and the poor debtor managed to get carried aboard it in a barrel. This barrel came from his farm and was supposed to contain provisions, and it was not till they were far away from land that it was opened and a living man was found in it instead of salt beef or pork.

When the captain saw him he was much astonished. He had paid for a barrel of provisions, and he found something which he could not well eat. He grew so angry at being cheated that he threatened to leave Balboa on a desert island, but the poor fellow got on his knees and begged so hard for his life that the captain at length forgave him. But he made him work to pay his way, and very likely used the rope's end to stir him up.

Of course you have learned from your geographies where the Isthmus of Darien (now called Panama) is, that narrow strip of land that is like a string tying together the great continents of North and South America. It was to the town of Darien, on this isthmus, that the ship made its way, and here Balboa made a surprising discovery. Some of the Indian chiefs told him of a mighty ocean which lay on the other side of the isthmus, and that beyond that ocean was the wonderful land of gold which the Spaniards wished to find.

What would you have done if you had been in Balboa's place, and wanted gold to pay your debts? Some of you, I think, would have done what he did. You would have made your way into the thick forest and climbed the rugged mountains of the isthmus, until, like Balboa, you got to the top of the highest peak. And, like him, you would have been filled with joy when you saw in the far distance the vast Pacific ocean, its waves glittering in the summer sun.

Here was glory; here was fortune. The poor debtor had become a great discoverer. Before his eyes spread a mighty ocean, its waves beating on the shore. He hurried with his men down the mountain sides to this shining sea, and raised on its shores the great banner of Spain. And soon after he set sail on its waters for Peru, the land of gold. But he did not get very far, for the stormy weather drove him back.

Poor Balboa! he was to win fame, but not fortune, and his debts were never to be paid. A jealous Spanish governor seized him, condemned him as a traitor, and had his head cut off in the market place. And so ended Balboa's dream of gold and glory. I could tell you of other wonderful adventures in these new lands. There is the story of Cortez, who found the great kingdom of Mexico, and conquered it with a few hundred Spaniards in armor of steel. And there is the story of Pizarro, who sailed to Peru, Balboa's land of gold, and won it for Spain, and sent home tons of silver and gold. But these stories have nothing to do with the history of the United States, so we must pass them by and go back to the early days of the country in which we dwell.

The first Spaniard to set foot on what is now the United States was an old man named Ponce de Leon, who was governor of Porto Rico. If he had lived until now he would have been on our soil while on that island, for it now belongs to the United States. But no one had dreamed of our great republic four hundred years ago.

At that time there was a fable which many believed, which said that somewhere in Asia was a wonderful Fountain of Youth. It was thought that everybody who bathed in its waters would grow young again. An old man in a moment would become as fresh and strong as a boy. De Leon wanted youth more than he did gold, and like all men at that time he thought the land he was in was part of Asia, and might contain the Fountain of Youth. He asked the Indians if they knew of such a magic spring. The red men, who wanted to get rid of the Spaniards, by whom they had been cruelly treated, pointed to the northwest.

So, in the year 1513, old Ponce de Leon took ship and sailed away in search of the magic spring. And not many days passed before, on Easter Sunday, he saw before him a land so bright with flowers that he named it "Flowery Easter." It is still called Florida, the Spanish word for "flowery."

I am sure none of my young readers believe in such a Fountain of Youth, and that none of you would have hunted for it as old De Leon did. Up and down that flowery land he wandered, seeking its wonderful waters. He found many sparkling springs, and eagerly drank of and bathed in their cool, liquid waves, but out of them all he came with white hair and wrinkled face. In the end he gave up the search, and sailed away, a sad old man. Some years afterwards he came back again. But this time the Indians fought with the white men, and De Leon was struck with an arrow, and hurt so badly that he soon died. So he found death instead of youth. Many people go to Florida in our own days in search of health, but Ponce de Leon is the only man who ever went there to find the magical Fountain of Youth.

About twenty-five years afterwards another Spaniard came to Florida. It was gold and glory he was after, not youth. This man, Fernando de Soto, had been in Peru with Pizarro, and helped him to conquer that land of gold. He now hoped to find a rich empire for himself in the north.

So with nine ships and six hundred brave young men he sailed away from his native land. They were a gay and hopeful band, while their bright banners floated proudly from the mastheads, and waved in the western winds. Little did they dream of what a terrible fate lay before them.

I think you will say that De Soto deserved a bad fate when I tell you that he brought bloodhounds to hunt the poor Indians, and chains to fasten on their hands and feet. That was the way the Spaniards often treated the poor red men. He brought also two hundred horses for his armed men to ride, and a drove of hogs to serve them for fresh meat. And in the ships were great iron chests, which he hoped to take back full of gold and other precious things.

For two long years De Soto and his band traveled through the country, fighting Indians, burning their houses and robbing them of their food. But the Indians were brave warriors, and in one terrible battle the Spaniards lost eighty of their horses and many of their men.

In vain De Soto sought for gold and glory. Not an ounce of the yellow metal was found; no mighty empire was reached. He did make one great discovery, that of the vast Mississippi River. But he never got home to tell of it, for he died on its banks, worn out with his battles and marches, and was buried under its waters. His men built boats and floated down the great river to the Gulf of Mexico. Here, at length, they found Spanish settlements. But of that brave and gallant band half were dead, and the rest were so nearly starved that they were like living skeletons.

We must not forget that humble Italian traveler and explorer, Amerigo Vespucci, who in 1499, saw the part of South America where lies the island of Trinidad. He afterwards reached the coast of Brazil. Some years later, when maps were made of the country he had visited, some one called it *America*. In later years this name was used for the whole continent. So what should have been called Columbia came to be called America.

CHAPTER III

THREE EARLY HEROES

WHAT do you think of Captain John Smith, the hero of Virginia? Was he not a man to dream of, a true hero? Why, I feel half ashamed to say anything about him, for every one of you must know his story. I am sure all those who love good stories of adventure have read about him.

John Smith was not the kind of man to work at a trade. He ran away from home when a boy, and became a wanderer over the earth. And a hard life he had of it. At one place he was robbed, and at another place was shipwrecked. Once he leaped overboard from a ship and swam ashore. Once again he fought with three Turks and killed all of them without help. Then he was taken prisoner, and sold as a slave to a cruel Turk, who put a ring round his neck and made him work very hard.

One day his master came out where he was at work and struck him with his whip. He soon found that John Smith was a bad man to whip. He hit the Turk a hard blow with the flail he was using, and killed him on the spot. Then he ran away, got to Russia, and in time made his way back to England. But England was too quiet a place for him. A ship was about to cross the sea to America and he volunteered to go in it. He had not half enough of adventure yet. Some people think that Captain Smith bragged a little, and did not do all he said. Well, that may be so. But it is certain that he was a brave and bold man, and just the man to help settle a new country where there were savage red men to deal with.

The English were in no hurry in sending out settlers to the New World which Columbus had discovered. While the Spaniards were seeking gold and empires in the south, and the French were catching fish and exploring the rivers and lakes in the north, all the English did was to rob the Spanish ships and settlements, and to bring them negroes from Africa for slaves.

But the time came, a hundred years after America was discovered, when some of the English tried to form a settlement on the coast of North Carolina. Poor settlers! When the next ship came out they were all gone. Not a soul of them could be found. Nothing was left but some letters they had cut into the bark of a tree. What became of them nobody ever knew. Likely enough they wandered away and were killed by the Indians.

Nothing more was done until the year 1607, when the ship in which Captain John Smith had taken passage sailed up a bright and beautiful river in Virginia. It was the month of May, and the banks were covered with flowers.

The colonists thought this a very good place to live in, so they landed and began to look around them. The river they called the James, and the place they named Jamestown. But instead of building a town and preparing for the future, as sensible men would have done, they began to seek for gold, and soon they were in no end of trouble. In a short time their food was all eaten. Then some of them were taken sick and died. Others were killed by the Indians. It looked as if this colony would come to grief as did the former one.

So it would if it had not been for Captain Smith. He was only one man among a hundred, but he was worth more than all the rest of the hundred. He could not keep still, but hustled about, here, there and everywhere. Now he was exploring the country, sailing up the rivers or up the broad Chesapeake Bay. Now he was talking with the Indians, getting food from them for the starving colonists. Now he was doing his best to make the men build houses and dig and plant the ground. You can see that John Smith had enough to keep him busy. He had many adventures with the Indians. At one time he was taken prisoner by them and was in terrible danger of being killed. But he showed them his pocket compass, and when they saw the needle always pointing north, they thought there must be magic in it. They were still more surprised when he sent one of them with a letter to his friends. They did not understand how a piece of paper could talk, as his paper seemed to do.

But all this was not enough to save his life. The great chief Powhatan looked on him as the leader of these white strangers who had settled in his land. He wanted to get rid of them, and thought that if he killed the man of the magic needle and the talking paper they would certainly be scared and go away.

So Captain Smith was tied hand and foot, and laid on the ground with his head on a log. And a powerful Indian stood near by with a great war club in his hand. Only a sign from Powhatan was needed, and down would come that club on the white man's head, and it would be all over with the brave and bold John Smith.

Alas! poor Captain Smith! There was no pity in Powhatan's eyes. The burly Indian twisted his fingers about the club and lifted it in the air. One minute more and it might be all over with the man who had killed three Turks in one fight. But before that minute was over a strange thing took place. A young Indian girl came running wildly toward him, with her hair flying and her eyes wet with tears. And she flung herself on the ground and laid her head on that of the bound prisoner, and begged the chief to give him his life.

It was Pocahontas, the pretty young daughter of Powhatan. She pleaded so pitifully that the chief's heart was touched, and he consented that the captive should live, and bade them take the bonds from his limbs.

Do you not think this a very pretty story? Some say that it is not true, but I think very likely it is. At any rate, it is so good that it ought to be true. Afterwards this warm-hearted Indian princess married one of the Virginians named John Rolfe and was taken to London and shown to the Queen. I am sorry to have to say that poor Pocahontas died there and never saw her native land again.

Captain Smith got safely back to Jamestown. But his troubles were not at an end, for the colonists were as hard to deal with as the Indians. Some of them had found a kind of yellow stuff which they were sure was gold. They loaded a ship with this and sent it to England, thinking that they would all be rich. But the yellow stuff proved to be what is known as "a fool's gold," and worth no more than so much sand. Instead of becoming rich, they were laughed at as great fools.

After a while Smith was made governor, and he now tried a new plan to make the men work. He told them that if they did not work they should not eat. None of them wanted to starve, and they knew that John Smith meant just what he said, so they began to build houses and to dig the ground and plant crops. But some of them grumbled and some of them swore, and it was anything but a happy family.

Captain Smith did not like this swearing, and he took a funny way to stop it. When the men came home at night each one who had sworn had a can of cold water poured down his sleeve for every time he had done so. Did any of my readers ever try that? If they did they would know why the men soon quit grumbling and swearing. All was beginning to go well in the colony when Captain Smith was hurt by some gunpowder that took fire and went off. He was hurt so badly that he had to go back to England. After that all went ill.

As soon as their governor was gone the lazy men quit working. The profane men swore worse than before. They ate up all their food in a hurry, and the Indians would bring them no more. Sickness and hunger came and carried many of them to the grave. Some of them meddled with the Indians and were killed. There were five hundred of them when winter set in; but when spring came only sixty of them were alive. And all this took place because one wise man, Captain John Smith, was hurt and had to go home.

The whole colony would have broken up if ships had not come out with more men and plenty of food. Soon after that, the people began to plant the ground and raise tobacco, which sold well in England. Many of them became rich, and the little settlement at Jamestown in time grew into the great colony of Virginia.

This ends the story of the hero of Jamestown. Now let us say something about the hero of Plymouth. In the year 1620, thirteen years after Smith and his fellows sailed up the James River, a shipload of men and women came to a place called Plymouth, on the rocky coast of New England. It was named Plymouth by Captain Smith, who had been there before. A portion of the rock on which they first stepped, is still preserved and surrounded by a fence.

These people are known as Pilgrims. They had been badly treated at home because they did believe in the teachings of the Church of England, and they had come across the stormy sea to find a place where they could worship God in their own way, without fear of being put in prison.

With them came a soldier. He was named Captain Miles Standish. He was a little man, but he carried a big sword, and had a stout heart and a hot temper. While the Pilgrims came to work and to pray, Captain Standish came to fight. He was a different man from Captain Smith, and would not have been able to deal with the lazy folks at Jamestown. But the Pilgrims were different also. They expected to work and live by their labor, and they had no sooner landed on Plymouth Rock than they began to dig and plant, while the sound of the hammer rang merrily all day long, as they built houses and got ready for the cold winter. But after all their labor and carefulness, sickness and hunger came, as they had come to Jamestown, and by the time the winter was over, half the poor Pilgrims were dead.

The Indians soon got to be afraid of Captain Standish. They were afraid of the Pilgrims, too, for they found that these religious men could fight as well as pray. One Indian chief, named Canonicus, sent them a bundle of arrows with a snake's skin tied round it. This was their way of saying that they were going to fight the Pilgrims and drive them from the country. But Governor Bradford filled the snake skin with powder and bullets and sent it back. When Canonicus saw this he was badly scared, for he knew well what it meant. He had heard the white men's guns, and thought they had the power of using thunder and lightning. So he made up his mind to let the white strangers alone.

But the Pilgrims did not trust the red men. They put cannon on the roof of their log church, and they walked to church on Sunday like so many soldiers on the march, with guns in their hands and Captain Standish at their head. And while they were listening to the sermon one man stood outside on the lookout for danger.

At one time some of the Indians made a plot to kill all the English. A friendly Indian told Captain Standish about it, and he made up his mind to teach them a lesson they would remember. He went to the Indian camp with a few men, and walked boldly into the hut where the plotting chiefs were talking over their plans. When they saw him and the men with him, they tried to frighten them. One of them showed the captain his knife and talked very boldly about it.

A big Indian looked with scorn on the little captain. "Pah, you are only a little fellow, if you are a captain," he said. "I am not a chief, but I am strong and brave."

Captain Standish was very angry, but he said nothing then. He waited until the next day, when he met the chiefs again. Then there was a quarrel and a fight, and the little captain killed the big Indian with his own knife. More of the Indians were slain, and the others ran for the woods. That put an end to the plot.

There is one funny story told about Captain Standish. His wife had died, and he felt so lonely that he wanted another; so he picked out a pretty young woman named Priscilla Mullins. But the rough old soldier knew more about fighting than about making love, and he sent his young friend, John Alden, to make love for him.

John told Priscilla's father what he had come for, and the father told Priscilla what John had told him. The pretty Priscilla had no fancy for the wrinkled old soldier. She looked at her father. Then she looked at John. Then she said: "Why don't you speak for yourself, John?"

John did speak for himself, and Priscilla became his wife. As for the captain, he married another woman, and this time I fancy he "spoke for himself."

Miles Standish lived to be 70 years old, and to have a farm of his own and a house on a high hill near Plymouth. This is called Captain's Hill, and on it there is now a stone shaft a hundred feet high, with a statue of bold Captain Standish on its top.

We have now our third hero to speak of, Roger Williams. He was not a captain like the others, but a preacher; but he was a brave man, and showed in his way as much courage as either of the captains.

The Pilgrims were quickly followed by other people, who settled at Boston and other places around Massachusetts Bay until there were a great many of them. These were called Puritans. They came across the seas for the same reason as the Pilgrims, to worship God in their own way.

But they were as hard to live with as the people at home, for they wanted to force everybody else into their way. Some Quakers who came to Boston were treated very badly because they had different ways from the Puritans. And one young minister named Roger Williams, who thought every man should have the right to worship as he pleased, and said that the Indians had not been treated justly, had to flee into the woods for safety.

It was winter time. The trees were bare of leaves and the ground was white with snow. Poor Roger had to wander through the cold woods, making a fire at night with his flint and steel, or sometimes creeping into a hollow tree to sleep.

Thus he went on, half frozen and half starved, for eighty long miles, to the house of Massasoit, an Indian chief who was his friend. The good chief treated him well, for he knew, like all the Indians, what Roger Williams had tried to do for them. When spring time came, Massasoit gave his guest a canoe and told him where to go. So Roger paddled away till he found a good place to stop. This place he called Providence. A large city now stands there, and is still called Providence.

Roger Williams had some friends with him, and others soon came, and after a few years he had quite a settlement of his own. It was called Rhode Island. Such a settlement as that at Plymouth, at Boston, and at Providence, was called "a colony."

He took care that the Indians should be treated well, and that no one should do them any harm, so they grew to love the good white man. And he said that every man in his colony should worship God in the way he liked best, and no one should suffer on account of his manner of worship.

It was a wonderful thing in those days, when there were wars going on in Europe about religion or the manner of worship, and everybody was punished who did not believe in the religion of the state.

Do you not think that Roger Williams was as brave a man as John Smith or Miles Standish, and as much of a hero? He did not kill any one. He was not that kind of a hero. But he did much to make men happy and good and to do justice to all men, and I think that is the best kind of a hero.

CHAPTER IV

THE DUTCH AND THE QUAKERS COME TO AMERICA

I WONDER how many of my readers have ever seen the great city of New York. I wonder still more how many of them knew that it is the largest city in the world except London. But we must remember that London is ten times as old, so it can well afford to be larger.

Why, if you should go back no farther than the time of your great-grandfather you would find no city of New York. All you would see would be a sort of large village on Manhattan Island, at the mouth of the Hudson River. And if you went back to the time of your grandfather's great-grandfather, I fancy you would see nothing on that island but trees, with Indian wigwams beneath them. Not a single white man or a single house would you see.

In the year 1609, just two years after Captain Smith sailed into the James River, a queer-looking Dutch vessel came across the ocean and began to prowl up and down the coast. It was named the "Half Moon." It came from Holland, the land of the Dutch, but its captain was an Englishman named Henry Hudson, who had done so many daring things that men called him "the bold Englishman."

What Captain Hudson would have liked to do was to sail across the United States and come out into the Pacific Ocean, and so make his way to the rich countries of Asia. Was not that a funny notion? To think that he could sail across three thousand miles of land and across great ranges of mountains!

But you must not think that Captain Hudson was crazy. Nobody then knew how wide America was. For all they knew, it might not be fifty miles wide. Captain John Smith tried to get across it by sailing up James River. And Captain Hudson fancied he might find some stream that led from one ocean to the other.

So on he went up and down the coast looking for an opening. And after a while the "Half Moon" sailed into a broad and beautiful bay, where great trees came down to the edge of the water and red men paddled about in their canoes. Captain Hudson was delighted to see it. "It was," he said, "as pleasant with grass and flowers as he had ever seen, and very sweet smells."

This body of water was what we now call New York Bay. A broad and swift river runs into it, which is now called Hudson River, after Henry Hudson. The bold captain thought that this was the stream to go up if he wished to reach the Pacific Ocean. So, after talking as well as he could with the Indians in their canoes, and trading beads for corn, he set his sails again and started up the splendid river. Some of the Indians came on board the "Half Moon," and the Dutch gave them brandy, which they had never seen or tasted before. Soon they were dancing and capering about the deck, and one of them fell down so stupid with drink that his friends thought he was dead. That was their first taste of the deadly "fire water" of the whites, which has killed thousands of the red men since then.

Captain Hudson and the Dutch no doubt thought that this was great fun. People often do much harm without stopping to think. But on up the river went the "Half Moon."

At some places they saw fields of green corn on the water's edge. Farther on were groves of lofty trees, and for miles great cliffs of rock rose like towers. It was all very grand and beautiful.

"It was a very good land to fall in with," said Captain Hudson, "and a pleasant land to see."

As they sailed on and on, they came to mountains, which rose on both sides the river. After passing the mountains, the captain went ashore to visit an old chief, who lived in a round house built of bark. The Indians here had great heaps of corn and beans. But what they liked best was roast dog. They roasted a dog for Captain Hudson and asked him to eat it, but I do not know whether he did so or not. And they broke their arrows and threw them into the fire, to show that they did not mean to do harm to the white men.

After leaving the good old chief the Dutch explorers went on up the river till they reached a place about 150 miles above the sea, where the city of Albany now stands. Here the river became so narrow and shallow that Captain Hudson saw he could not reach the Pacific by that route, so he turned and sailed back to the sea again.

A sad fate was that of Captain Hudson, "the bold Englishman." The next year he came again to America. But this time he went far to the north and entered the great body of water which we call Hudson Bay. He thought this would lead to the Pacific, and he would not turn back, though the food was nearly all gone. At last the crew got desperate, and they put the captain and some others into an open boat on the wide waters, and turned back again. Nothing more was ever heard of Captain Hudson, and he must have died miserably on that cold and lonely bay.

But before his last voyage he had told the Dutch people all about Hudson River, and that the Indians had many fine furs which they would be glad to trade for beads, and knives, and other cheap things. The Dutch were fond of trading, and liked to make a good bargain, so they soon began to send ships to America. They built a fort and some log huts on Manhattan Island, and a number of them stayed there to trade with the red men. They paid the Indians for the island with some cheap goods worth about twenty-four dollars. I do not think any of you could guess how many millions of dollars that island is worth now. For the great city of New York stands where the log huts of the Dutch traders once stood, and twenty-four dollars would hardly buy as much land as you could cover with your hand.

The country around is now all farming land, where grain and fruit are grown, and cattle are raised. But then it was all woodland for hundreds of miles away, and in these woods lived many foxes and beavers and other fur-bearing animals. These the Indians hunted and killed, and sold their furs to the Dutch, so that there was soon a good trade for both the red and the white men. The Dutch were glad to get the furs and the Indians were as glad to get the knives and beads. More and more people came from Holland, and the town grew larger and larger, and strong brick houses took the place of the log huts, and in time there was quite a town.

Men were sent from Holland to govern the people. Some of these men were not fit to govern themselves, and the settlers did not like to have such men over them. One of them was a stubborn old fellow named Peter Stuyvesant. He had lost one of his legs, and wore a wooden leg with bands of silver around it, so that he was called "Old Silver Leg."

While he was governor an important event took place. The English had a settlement in Virginia and another in New England, and they said that all the coast lands belonged to them, because the Cabots had been the first to see them. The Cabots came from Italy, but they had settled in England, and sailed in an English ship.

So one day a small fleet of English vessels came into the bay, and a letter was sent on shore which said that all this land belonged to England and must be given up to them. The Dutch might stay there, but they would be under an English governor. Old Peter tore up the letter and stamped about in a great rage on his silver leg. But he had treated the people so badly that they would not fight for him, so he had to give up the town.

The English called it New York, after the Duke of York, the king's brother. It grew and grew till it became a great and rich city, and sent ships to all parts of the world. Most of the Dutch stayed there, and their descendants are among the best people of New York to-day. Not long after these English ships came to New York Bay, other English ships came to a fine body of water, about 100 miles farther south, now called Delaware Bay. Into this also runs a great stream of fresh water, called Delaware River, as wide as the Hudson. I think you will like to learn what brought them here.

No doubt you remember what I said about some people called Quakers, who came to Boston and were treated very badly by the Puritans. Did any of my young readers ever see a Quaker? In old times you would have known them, for they dressed in a different way from other people. They wore very plain clothes and broad-brimmed hats, which they would not take off to do honor to king or noble. To-day they generally dress more like the people around them.

If they were treated badly in Boston they were treated worse in England. Thieves and highwaymen had as good a time as the poor Quakers. Some of them were put in jail and kept there for years. Some were whipped or put in the stocks, where low people called them vile names and threw mud at them. Indeed, these quiet people, who did no harm to any one, but were kind to others, had a very hard time, and were treated more cruelly than the Pilgrims and the Puritans.

Among them was the son of a brave English admiral, who was a friend of the king and his brother, the Duke of York. But this did not save him from being put in prison for preaching as a Quaker and wearing his hat in court.

This was William Penn, from whom Pennsylvania was named. You may well fancy that the son of a rich admiral and the friend of a king did not like being treated as though he were a thief because he chose to wear a hat with a broad brim and to say "thee" and "thou," and because he would not go to the king's church.

What is more, the king owed him money, which he could not or would not pay. He had owed this money to Admiral Penn, and after the admiral died he owed it to his son.

William Penn thought it would be wise to do as the Pilgrims and Puritans had done. There was plenty of land in America, and it would be easy there to make a home for the poor Quakers where they could live in peace and worship God in the way they thought right. This they could not do in England.

Penn went to the king and told him how he could pay his debt. If the king would give him a tract of land on the west side of the Delaware River, he would take it as payment in full for the money owing to his father.

King Charles, who never had money enough for his own use, was very glad to pay his debts in this easy way. He told Penn that he could have all the land he wanted, and offered him a tract that was nearly as large as the whole of England. This land belonged to the red men, but that did not trouble King Charles. It is easy to pay debts in other people's property. All Penn was asked to pay the king was two beaver skins every year and one-fifth of all the gold and silver that should be mined. As no gold or silver was ever mined the king got nothing but his beaver skins, which were a kind of rent.

What do any of my young readers know about the Delaware River? Have any of you seen the wide, swift stream which flows between the states of Pennsylvania and New Jersey, and runs into the broad body of water known as Delaware Bay? On its banks stands the great city of Philadelphia, in which live more than a million people, and where there are thousands of busy workshops and well-filled stores. This large and fine city came from the way the king paid his debt. King Charles was not a good man, but he did one thing that had a good ending.

There were white men there before the Quakers came. Many years earlier a number of people from Sweden had come and settled along the river. Then the Dutch from New York said the land was theirs, and took possession of the forts of the Swedes. Then the English of New York claimed the land as theirs. Then Quakers came and settled in New Jersey. Finally came William Penn, in a ship called by the pretty name of the "Welcome," and after that the land was governed by the Quakers or Friends, though the Swedes stayed there still.

We have something very pleasant to say about good William Penn. He knew very well that King Charles did not own the land, and had no right to sell it or give it away. So he called the Indians together under a great elm tree on the river bank, and had a long talk with them, and told them he would pay them for all the land he wanted. This pleased the red men very much, and ever afterwards they loved William Penn.

Do you not think it must have been a pretty scene when Penn and the Quakers met the Indian chiefs under the great tree—the Indians in their colored blankets and the Quakers in their great hats? That tree stood for more than a hundred years afterwards, and when the British army was in Philadelphia during the war of the Revolution their general put a guard around Penn's treaty tree, so that the soldiers should not cut it down for firewood. The tree is gone now, but a stone monument marks where it stood. A city was laid out on the river, which Penn named Philadelphia, a word which means Brotherly Love. I suppose some brotherly love is there still, but not nearly so much as there should be.

Streets were made through the woods, and the names of the trees were given to these streets, which are still known as Chestnut, Walnut, Pine, Cherry, and the like. People soon came in numbers, and it is wonderful how fast the city grew. Soon there were hundreds of comfortable houses, and in time it grew to be the largest in the country.

The Indians looked on in wonder to see large houses springing up where they had hunted deer, and to see great ships where they had paddled their canoes. But the white men spread more and more into the land, and the red men were pushed back, and in time none of them were left in Penn's woodland colony. This was long after William Penn was dead.

But while Penn's city was growing large and rich, he was becoming poor. He spent much money on his province and got very little back. At last he became so poor that he was put in prison for debt, as was the custom in those days. In the end he died and left the province to his sons. The Indians sent some beautiful furs to his widow in memory of their great and good brother. They said these were to make her a cloak "to protect her while she was passing without her guide through the stormy wilderness of life."

CHAPTER V

THE CAVALIER COLONIES OF THE SOUTH

VIRGINIA has often been called the Cavalier colony. Do any of you know why, or who the Cavaliers were? Perhaps I had better tell you. They were the lords and the proud people of England. Many of them had no money, but they would do no work, and cared for nothing but pleasure and fighting. There were plenty of working people in that country, but there were many who were too proud to work, and expected others to work for them, while they hoped to live at ease.

Some of this kind of men came out with John Smith, and that is why he had so much trouble with them. The Puritans and the Quakers came from the working people of England, and nobody had to starve them to make them work, or to pour cold water down their sleeves to stop them from swearing.

While religious people settled in the North, many of the proud Cavalier class, who cared very little about religion, came to the South. So we may call the southern settlements the Cavalier colonies, though many of the common people came there too, and it was not long before there was plenty of work.

The first to come after John Smith and the Jamestown people were some shiploads of Catholics. You should know that the Catholics were treated in England even worse than the Puritans and the Quakers. The law said they must go to the English Church instead of to their own. If they did not they would have to pay a large sum of money or go to prison. Was not this very harsh and unjust?

The Catholics were not all poor people. There were rich men and nobles among them. One of these nobles, named Lord Baltimore, asked the King for some land in America where he and his friends might dwell in peace and have churches of their own. This was many years before William Penn asked for the same thing. The King was a friend of Lord Baltimore and told him he might have as much land as he could make use of. So he chose a large tract just north of Virginia, which the King named Maryland, after his wife, Queen Mary, who was a Catholic. All Lord Baltimore had to pay for this was two Indian arrows every year, and a part of the gold and silver, if any were found. This was done to show that the King still kept some claim to Maryland, and did not give away all his rights.

And now comes a story much the same as I have told you several times already. A shipload of Catholics and other people came across the ocean to the new continent which Columbus had discovered many years before. These sailed up the broad Chesapeake Bay. You may easily find this bay on your maps. They landed at a place they called St. Mary's, where there was a small Indian town. As it happened, the Indians at this town had been so much troubled by fighting tribes farther north that they were just going to move somewhere else. So they were very glad to sell their town to the white strangers.

All they wanted for their houses and their corn fields were some hatchets, knives and beads, and other things they could use. Gold and silver would have been of no value to them, for they had never seen these metals. The only money the Indians used was round pieces of seashell, with holes bored through them. Before these people left their town they showed the white men how to hunt in the woods and how to plant corn. And their wives taught the white women how to make hominy out of corn and how to bake johnny-cakes. So the people of Maryland did not suffer from hunger like those of Virginia and New England, and they had plenty to eat and lived very well from the start.

This was in the year 1634, just about the time Roger Williams went to Rhode Island. Lord Baltimore did the same thing that Roger Williams did; he gave the people religious liberty. Every Christian who came to Maryland had the right to worship God in his own way. Roger Williams went farther than this, for he gave the same right to Jews and all other people, whether they were Christians or pagans.

It was not long before other people came to Maryland, and they began to plant tobacco, as the people were doing in Virginia. Tobacco was a good crop to raise, for it could be sold for a high price in England, so that the Maryland planters did very well, and many of them grew rich. But religious liberty did not last there very long, and the Catholics were not much better off than they had been in England. All the poor people who came with Lord Baltimore were Protestants. Only the rich ones were Catholics. Many other Protestants soon came, some of them being Puritans from New England, who did not know what religious liberty meant.

These people said that the Catholics should not have the right to worship in their own churches, even in Maryland, and they went so far that they tried to take from Lord Baltimore the lands which the king had given him. There was much fighting between the Catholics and the Protestants. Now one party got the best of it, and now the other. In the end the province was taken from Lord Baltimore's son; and when a new king, named King William, came to the throne, he said that Maryland was his property, and that the Catholics should not have a church of their own or worship in their own way in that province. Do you not think this was very cruel and unjust? It seems so to me. It did not seem right, after Lord Baltimore had given religious liberty to all men, for others to come and take it away. But the custom in those days was that all men must be made to think the same way, or be punished if they didn't. This seems queer now-a-days, when every man has the right to think as he pleases.

In time there was born a Lord Baltimore who became a Protestant, and the province was given back to him. It grew rich and full of people, and large towns were built. One of these was named Baltimore, after Lord Baltimore, and is now a great city. And Washington, the capital of the United States, stands on land that was once part of Maryland. But St. Mary's, the first town built, has gone, and there is hardly a mark left to show where it stood.

Maryland, as I have said, lies north of Virginia. The Potomac River runs between them. South of Virginia was another great tract of land, reaching all the way to Florida, which the Spaniards then held. Some French Protestants tried to settle there, but they were cruelly murdered by the Spaniards, and no one else came there for many years.

About 1660 people began to settle in what was then called "the Carolinas," but is now called North Carolina and South Carolina. Some of these came from Virginia and some from England, and small settlements were made here and there along the coast. One of these was called Charleston. This has now grown into a large and important city.

There were some noblemen in England who thought that this region might become worth much money, so they asked the king, Charles II., to give it to them. This was the same king who gave the Dutch settlement to the Duke of York and who afterwards gave Pennsylvania to William Penn. He was very ready to give away what did not belong to him, and told these noblemen that they were welcome to the Carolinas. There were eight of these men, and they made up their minds that they would have a very nice form of government for their new province. So they went to a famous man named John Locke, who was believed to be very wise, and asked him to draw up a form of government for them.

John Locke drew up a plan of government which they thought very fine, but which everybody now thinks was very foolish and absurd. I fancy he knew more about books than he did about government. He called it the "Grand Model," and the noble lords thought they had a wonderful government indeed. There were to be earls, and barons, and lords, the same as in Europe. No one could vote who did not hold fifty acres. The poorer people were to be like so many slaves. They could not even leave one plantation for another without asking leave from the lord or baron who owned it.

What do you think the people did? You must not imagine they came across the ocean to be made slaves of. No, indeed! They cared no more for the "Grand Model" than if it was a piece of tissue paper. They settled where they pleased, and would not work for the earls and barons, and fought with the governors, and refused to pay the heavy taxes which the eight noble owners asked.

In time these noblemen got so sick of the whole business that they gave their province back to the king. It was then divided into two colonies, known as North Carolina and South Carolina. As for the lords and barons, nobody heard of them any more.

The people of the Carolinas had other things beside the Grand Model of government to trouble them. There were savage Indians back in the country who attacked them and killed many of them. And there were pirates along the coast who attacked ships and killed all on board. But rice and indigo were planted, and afterwards cotton, and much tar and turpentine were got from the pine trees in North Carolina, and as the years went on these colonies became rich and prosperous, and the people began to have a happy time.

I hope none of my young readers are tired of reading about kings and colonies. I am sure they must have enjoyed reading about John Smith and Miles Standish and William Penn and the rest of the great leaders. At any rate, there is only one more colony to talk about, and then we will be through with this part of our story. This is the colony of Georgia, which lies in the tract of land between South Carolina and Florida.

I am sure that when you are done reading this book you will be glad that you did not live two or three hundred years ago. To-day every one can think as he pleases, and do as he pleases, too, if he does not break the laws. And the laws are much more just and less cruel than they were in former times. Why, in those days, every man who owed money and could not pay it might be put in prison and kept there for years. He could not work there and earn money to pay his debts, and if his friends did not pay them he might stay there till he died. As I have told you, even the good William Penn was put in prison for debt, and kept there till his friends paid the money.

There were as many poor debtors in prison as there were thieves and villains. Some of them become sick and died, and some were starved to death by cruel jailers, who would not give them anything to eat if they had no money to pay for food. One great and good man, named General James

Oglethorpe, visited the prisons, and was so sorry for the poor debtors he saw there, that he asked the king to give him a piece of land in America where he could take some of these suffering people.

There was now not much land left to give. Settlements had been made all along the coast except south of the Carolinas, and the king told General Oglethorpe that he could have the land which lay there, and could take as many debtors out of prison as he chose. He thought it would be a good thing to take them somewhere where they could work and earn their living. The king who was then on the throne was named King George, so Oglethorpe called his new colony Georgia.

It was now the year 1733, a hundred years after Lord Baltimore had come to Maryland. General Oglethorpe took many of the debtors out of prison, and very glad they were to get out, you may be sure. He landed with them on the banks of a fine river away down South, where he laid out a town which he named Savannah.

The happy debtors now found themselves in a broad and beautiful land, where they could prove whether they were ready to work or not. They were not long in doing this. Right away they began to cut down trees, and build houses, and plant fields, and very soon a pretty town was to be seen and food plants were growing in the fields. And very happy men and women these poor people were.

General Oglethorpe knew as well as William Penn that the land did not belong to the king. He sent for the Indian chiefs and told them the land was theirs, and offered to pay them for it. They were quite willing to sell, and soon he had all the land he wanted, and what is more, he had the Indians for friends.

But if he had no trouble with the Indians, he had a good deal with the Spaniards of Florida. They said that Georgia was a part of Florida and that the English had no right there. And they sent an army and tried to drive them out.

I fancy they did not know that Oglethorpe was an old soldier, but he soon showed them that he knew how to fight. He drove back their armies and took their ships; and they quickly made up their minds that they had better let the English alone. There was plenty of land for both, for the Spaniards had only one town in Florida. This was St. Augustine.

Before long some Germans came from Europe and settled in the new colony. People came also from other parts of Europe. Corn was planted for food, and some of the colonists raised silkworms and made silk. But in the end, cotton came to be the chief crop of the colony.

General Oglethorpe lived to be a very old man. He did not die till long after the American Revolution. Georgia was then a flourishing state, and the little town he had started on the banks of the Savannah River was a fine city, with broad streets, fine mansions, and beautiful shade trees. I think the old general must have been very proud of this charming city, and of the great state which owed its start to him.

CHAPTER VI

THE RED MEN, HOW THEY LIVED AND WERE TREATED

NOW that you have been told about the settlement of the colonies, it is well to recall how many of them there were. Let us see. There were the Pilgrim and Puritan settlements of New England, Roger Williams's settlement in Rhode Island, the Dutch settlement in New York, the Quaker one in Pennsylvania, the Catholic settlement in Maryland, the Cavalier ones in Virginia and the Carolinas, and the Debtor settlement in Georgia. Then there were some smaller ones, making about a dozen in all.

These stretched all along the coast, from Canada, the French country in the north, to Florida, the Spanish country in the south. The British were a long time in settling these places, for nearly 250 years passed after the time of Columbus before General Oglethorpe came to Georgia.

While all this was going on, what was becoming of the native people of the country, the Indians? I am afraid they were having a very hard time of it. The Spaniards made slaves of them, and forced them to work so terribly hard in the mines and the fields that they died by thousands. The French and the English fought with them and drove them away from their old homes, killing many of them.

And this has gone on and on ever since, until the red men, who once spread over all this country, are now kept in a very small part of it. Some people say there are as many of them as they ever were. If that is so, they can live on much less land than they once occupied.

What do you know about these Indians? Have you ever seen one of them? Your fathers or grandfathers have, I am sure, for once they were everywhere in this country, and people saw more of them than they liked; but now we see them only in the Wild West shows or the Indian schools, except we happen to go where they live. Do you not want to know something about these oldest Americans? I have been busy so far talking about the white men and what they did, and have had no chance to tell you about the people they found on this continent and how they treated them. I think I must make this chapter an Indian one.

Well, then, when the Spanish came to the south, and the French to the north, and the Dutch and the Swedes and the British to the middle country, they found everywhere a kind of people they had never seen before. Their skin was not white, like that of the people of Europe, nor black like that of the Africans, but of a reddish color, like that of copper, so that they called them red men. They had black eyes and hair, and high cheek-bones, and were not handsome according to our ideas; but they were tall and strong, and many of them very proud and dignified.

These people lived in a very wild fashion. They spent much of their time in hunting, fishing, and fighting. They raised some Indian corn and beans, and were fond of tobacco, but most of their food was got from wild animals killed in the woods. They were as fond of fighting as they were of hunting. They were divided into tribes, some of which were nearly always at war with other tribes. They had no weapons but stone hatchets and bows and arrows, but they were able with these to kill many of their enemies. People say that they were badly treated by the whites, but they treated one another worse than the whites ever did.

The Indians were very cruel. The warriors shaved off all their hair except one lock, which was called the scalp lock. When one of them was killed in battle this lock was used to pull off his scalp, or the skin of his head. They were very proud of these scalps, for they showed how many men they had killed.

When they took a prisoner, they would tie him to a tree and build a fire round him and burn him to death. And while he was burning they would torture him all they could. We cannot feel so much pity for the Indians when we think of all this. No doubt the white men have treated them very unjustly, but they have stopped all these terrible cruelties, and that is something to be thankful for. In this country, where once there was constant war and bloodshed, and torturing and burning of prisoners, now there is peace and kindness and happiness. So if evil has been done, good has come of it.

At the time I am speaking of, forests covered much of this great continent. They spread everywhere, and the Indians lived under their shade, and had wonderful skill in following animals or enemies through their shady depths. They read the ground much as we read the pages of a book. A broken twig, a bit of torn moss, a footprint which we could not see, were full of meaning to them, and they would follow a trail for miles through the woods where we would not have been able to follow it a yard. Their eyes were trained to this kind of work, but in time some of the white men became as expert as the Indians, and could follow a trail as well.

The red men lived mostly in little huts covered with skins or bark, which they called wigwams. Some of the tribes lived in villages, where there were large bark houses. But they did not stay much in their houses, for they liked better to be in the open air. Now they were hunting deer in the woods, now fishing or paddling their bark canoes in the streams, now smoking their pipes in front of their huts, now dancing their war dances or getting ready to fight.

The men did nothing except hunting and fighting. The women had to do all other work, such as cooking, planting and gathering corn, building wigwams, and the like. They did some weaving of cloth, but most of their clothes were made of the skins of wild animals.

In war times the warriors tried to make themselves as ugly as they could, painting their faces in a horrid fashion and sticking feathers in their hair. They seemed to think they could scare their enemies by ugly faces.

I have spoken of the tribes of the Indians. Some of these tribes were quite large, and were made up of a great number of men and women who lived together and spoke the same language. Each tribe was divided up into clans, or small family-like groups, and each clan had its sachem, or peace-chief. There were war-chiefs, also, who led them to battle. The sachems and chiefs governed the tribes and made such laws as they had.

Every clan had some animal which it called its totem, such as the wolf, bear, or fox. They were proud of their totems, and the form of the animal was tattooed on their breast; that is, it was picked into the skin with needles. All the Indians were fond of dancing, and their war dances were as fierce and wild as they could make them.

The tribes in the south were not as savage as those in the north. They did more farming, and had large and well-built villages. Some of them had temples and priests, and looked upon the sun as a god. They kept a fire always burning in the temple, and seemed to think this fire was a part of their sun-god. They had a great chief who ruled over the tribe, and also a head war-chief, a high-priest, and other rulers.

In the far west were Indians who built houses that were almost like towns, for they had hundreds of rooms. A whole tribe could live in one of these great houses, sometimes as many as three thousand people. Other tribes lived in holes in the sides of steep rocks, where their enemies could not easily get at them. These are called Cliff-dwellers. And there were some who lived on top of high, steep hills, which were very hard to climb. These Indians raised large crops of corn and other plants.

Do you think, if you had been an Indian, you would have liked to see white people coming in ships across the waters and settling down in your country as if they owned it? They did not all pay for the land they took, like William Penn and General Oglethorpe. The most of them acted as if the country belonged to them, and it is no wonder the old owners of the country did not like it, or that there was fierce fighting between the white and the red men.

Do you remember the story of Canonicus and the snake skin, and that of Miles Standish and the chiefs? There was not much fighting then, but there was some soon after in Connecticut, whither a number of settlers had come from Boston and others from England. Here there was a warlike tribe called the Pequots, who became very angry on seeing the white men in their country.

They began to kill the whites whenever they found them alone. Then the whites began to kill the Indians. Soon there was a deadly war. The Pequots had made a fort of trunks of trees, set close together in the ground. They thought they were safe in this fort, but the English made an attack on it, and got into it, and set fire to the Indian wigwams inside. The fight went on terribly in the smoke and flame until nearly all the Pequots were killed. Only two white men lost their lives. This so scared the Indians that it was forty years before there was another Indian war in New England.

I have told you about the good chief Massasoit, who was so kind to Roger Williams. He was a friend to the white men as long as he lived, but after his death his son Philip became one of their greatest enemies.

Philip's brother was taken sick and died after he had been to Plymouth, and the Indians thought that the people there had given him poison. Philip said that they would try to kill him next, and he made up his mind to fight them and drive them out of the country. The Indians had guns now, and knew how to use them, and they began to shoot the white people as they went quietly along the roads.

Next they began to attack the villages of the whites. They would creep up at night, set the houses on fire, and shoot the men as they came out. The war went on for a long time in this way, and there were many terrible fights.

At one place the people, when they saw the Indians coming, all ran to a strong building called a blockhouse. The Indians came whooping and yelling around this, and tried to set it on fire by shooting arrows with blazing rags on their points. Once the roof caught fire, but some of the men ran up and threw water on the flames.

Then the Indians got a cart and filled it with hay. Setting this on fire, they pushed it up against the house. It looked as if all the white men and women and children would be burned alive. The house caught fire and began to blaze. But just then came a shower of rain that put out the fire, and the people inside were saved once more. Before the Indians could do anything further some white soldiers came and the savages all ran into the woods.

There were other wonderful escapes, but many of the settlers were killed, and Philip began to think he would be able to drive them out of the country, as he wished to do. He was called King Philip, though he had no crown except a string of wampum,—or bits of bored shell strung together and twined round his head,—and no palace better than a bark hut, while his finest dress was a red blanket. It took very little to make an Indian king. The white men knew more about war than the Indians, and in the end they began to drive them back. One of their forts was taken, and the wigwams in it were set on fire, like those of the Pequots. A great many of the poor red men perished in the flames.

The best fighter among the white men was Captain Church. He followed King Philip and his men to one hiding place after another, killing some and taking others prisoners. Among the prisoners were the wife and little son of the Indian king.

"It breaks my heart," said Philip, when he heard of this. "Now I am ready to die."

He did not live much longer. Captain Church chased him from place to place, till he came to Mount Hope, in Rhode Island, where Massasoit lived when Roger Williams came to him through the woods. Here King Philip was shot, and the war ended. It had lasted more than a year, and a large number had been killed on both sides. It is known in history as King Philip's War.

There were wars with the Indians in many other parts of the country. In Virginia the Indians made a plot to kill all the white people. They pretended to be very friendly, and brought them meat and fish to sell. While they were talking quietly the savages drew their tomahawks or hatchets and began to kill the whites. In that one morning nearly three hundred and fifty were killed, men, women, and little children.

Hardly any of the settlers were left alive, except those in Jamestown, who were warned in time. They now attacked the Indians, shooting down all they could find, and killing a great many of them.

This was after the death of Powhatan, who had been a friend to the whites. About twenty years later, in 1644, another Indian massacre took place. After this the Indians were driven far back into the country, and did not give any more trouble for thirty years. The last war with them broke out in 1675.

The Dutch in New York also had their troubles with the Indians. They paid for all the lands they took, but one of their governors was foolish enough to start a war that went on for two years. A worse trouble was that in North Carolina, where there was a powerful tribe called the Tuscaroras. These attacked the settlers and murdered numbers of them. But in the end they were driven out of the country.

The only colonies in which the Indians kept friendly for a long time were Pennsylvania and Georgia. We know the reason of this. William Penn and General Oglethorpe were wise enough to make friends with them at the start, and continued to treat them with justice and friendliness, so that the red men came to love these good men.

CHAPTER VII

ROYAL GOVERNORS AND LOYAL CAPTAINS

DO any of my young readers know what is meant by a Charter? "Yes," I hear some of you say. "No," say others. Well, I must speak to the "No," party; the party that doesn't know, and wants to know.

A charter is a something written or printed which grants certain rights or privileges to the party to whom it is given. It may come from a king or a congress, or from any person in power, and be given to any other person who wishes the right to hold a certain property or to do some special thing.

Do you understand any better now? I am sorry I can not put it in plainer words. I think the best way will be to tell you about some charters which belong to American history. You should know that all the people who crossed the ocean to make new settlements on the Atlantic Coast had charters from the king of England. This was the case with the Pilgrims and the Puritans, with Roger Williams, William Penn, Lord Baltimore, and the others I have spoken about.

These charters were written on parchment, which is the skin of an animal, made into something like paper. The charters gave these people the right to settle on and own certain lands, to form certain kinds of government, and to do a variety of things which in England no one could do but the king and the parliament.

The colonies in New England were given the right to choose their own governors and make their own laws, and nobody, not even the king, could stop them from doing this. The king had given them this right, and no other king could take it away while they kept their charters.

Would you care to be told what took place afterwards? All kings, you should know, are not alike. Some are very mild and easy, and some are very harsh and severe. Some are willing for the people to have liberty, and some are not. The kings who gave the charters to New England were of the easy kind. But they were followed by kings of the hard kind, who thought that these people beyond the sea had too much liberty, and who wished to take away some of it.

Charles II., who gave some of these charters, was one of the easy kings, and did not trouble himself about the people in the colonies. James II., who came after him, was one of the hard kings. He was somewhat of a tyrant, and wanted to make the laws himself, and to take the right to do this from the people. After trying to rob the people of England of their liberties, he thought he would do the same thing with the people of America. "Those folks across the seas are having too good a time," he thought. "They have too many rights and privileges, and I must take some of them away. I will let them know that I am their master."

But they had their charters, which gave them these rights; so the wicked king thought the first thing for him to do was to take their charters away from them. Then their rights would be gone, and he could make for them a new set of laws, and force them to do everything he wished.

What King James did was to send a nobleman named Sir Edmund Andros to New England to rule as royal governor. He was the agent of the king, and was to do all that the king ordered. He began by undertaking to rob the people of their charters. You see, even a tyrant king did not like to go against the charters, for a charter was a sacred pledge.

Well, the new governor went about ordering the people to give him their charters. One of the places to which he went was Hartford, Connecticut, and there he told the officers of the colony that they must deliver up their charter; the king had said so, and the king's word must be obeyed.

If any of you had lived in Connecticut in those days I know how you would have felt. The charter gave the people a great deal of liberty, and they did not wish to part with it. I know that you and I would have felt the same way. But what could they do? If they did not give it up peacefully, Governor Andros might come again with soldiers and take it from them by force. So the lawmakers and officials were in a great fret about what they should do.

They asked Governor Andros to come to the State-house and talk over the matter. Some of them fancied they could get him to leave them their charter, though they might have known better. There they sat—the governor in the lofty chair of state, the others seated in a half circle before him. There was a broad table between them, and on this lay the great parchment of the charter. Some of those present did a great deal of talking. They told how good King Charles had given them the charter, and how happy they had been under it, and how loyal they were to good King James, and they begged Governor Andros not to take it from them. But they might as well have talked to the walls. He had his orders from the king and was one of the men who do just what they are told.

While the talk was going on a strange thing happened. It was night, and the room was lit up with a few tallow candles. Of course you know that these were the best lights people had at that time; gas or the electric light had never been heard of. And it was before the time of matches. The only way to make a light in those days was by the use of the flint and steel, which was a very slow method indeed.

Suddenly, while one of the Hartford men was talking and the governor was looking at him in a tired sort of way, all the lights in the room went out, and the room was in deep darkness. Everybody jumped up from their chairs and there was no end of bustle and confusion, and likely enough some pretty hard words were said. They had to hunt in the dark for the flint and steel; and then there came snapping of steel on flint, and falling of sparks on tinder, so that it was some time before the candles were lit again.

When this was done the governor opened his eyes very wide, for the table was empty, the charter was gone. I fancy he swore a good deal when he saw that. In those days even the highest people were given to swearing. But no matter how much he swore, he could not with hard words bring back the charter. It was gone, and nobody knew where. Everybody looked for it, right and left, in and out, in drawers and closets, but it was nowhere to be found. Very likely the most of them did not want to find it. At any rate, the governor had to go away without the charter, and years passed before anybody saw it again.

Do you not wish to know what became of it? We are told that it had been taken by a bold young soldier named Captain Wadsworth. While all the people in the room were looking at the one who was making his speech, the captain quickly took off his cloak and gave it a quick fling over the candles, so that in a moment they were all put out. Then he snatched up the charter from the table and slipped quietly out of the room. While they were busy snapping the flint and steel, he was hurrying down the street towards a great oak tree which was more than a hundred years old. This tree was hollow in its heart, and there was a hole in its side which opened into the hollow. Into this hole Captain Wadsworth pushed the charter, and it fell into the hollow space. I do not think any of us would have thought of looking there for it. I know nobody did at that time, and there it lay for years, until the tyrant King James was driven from the throne and a new king had taken his place. Then it was joyfully brought out, and the people were ever so glad to see it again.

The old tree stood for many years in the main street of the town, and became famous as the Charter Oak. The people loved and were proud of it as long as it stood. But many years ago the hoary old oak fell, and now only some of its wood is left. This has been made into chairs and boxes and other objects which are thought of great value.

Do you not think that Captain Wadsworth was a bold and daring man, and one who knew just what to do in times of trouble? If you do not, I fancy you will when I have told you another story about him.

This took place after the charter had been taken from the oak and brought to the statehouse again. At this time there was a governor in New York named Fletcher, who claimed that the king had given him the right to command the militia, or citizen soldiers, of Connecticut. So he came to Hartford, where Captain Wadsworth was in command, and where the people did not want any stranger to have power over them. He told the captain what he had come for, and that he had a commission to read to the soldiers.

The militia were called out and drawn up in line in the public square of the town, and Governor Fletcher came before them, full of his importance. He took out of his pocket the paper which he said gave him the right to command, and began to read it in a very proud and haughty manner. But he had not read ten words when Captain Wadsworth told the drummers to beat their drums, and before you could draw your breath there was such a rattle and roll of noise that not a word could be heard.

"Silence!" cried Fletcher. "Stop those drums!" The drums stopped, and he began to read again.

"Drum!" ordered Wadsworth in a loud tone, and such a noise began that a giant's voice would have been drowned.

"Silence!" again shouted Fletcher. He was very red in the face by this time.

"Drum, I say!" roared the captain.

Then he turned to the governor and said, laying his hand on his sword, "I command these men, Governor Fletcher, and if you interrupt me again I will make the sun shine through you in a minute." And he looked as if he meant what he said. All the governor's pomp and consequence were gone, and his face turned from red to pale. He hastily thrust the paper back into his pocket, and was not long in leaving Hartford for New York. No doubt he thought that Connecticut was not a good place for royal governors.

Suppose I now tell you the story of another royal governor and another bold captain. This was down in Virginia, but it was long after Captain Smith was dead and after Virginia had become a large and prosperous colony.

The king sent there a governor named Berkeley, who acted as if he was master and all the people were his slaves. They did not like to be treated this way; but Berkeley had soldiers under his command, and they were forced to obey. While this was going on the Indians began to murder the settlers. The governor ought to have stopped them, but he was afraid to call out the people, and he let the murders go on.

There was a young man named Nathaniel Bacon who asked Governor Berkeley to let him raise some men to fight the Indians. The governor refused. But this did not stop brave young Bacon, for he called out a force of men and drove off the murdering savages.

Governor Berkeley was very angry at this. He said that Bacon was a traitor and ought to be treated like one, and that the men with him were rebels. Bacon at once marched with his men against Jamestown, and the haughty governor ran away as fast as he could.

But while Bacon and his men were fighting the Indians again, Governor Berkeley came back and talked more than ever about rebels and traitors. This made Bacon and the people with him very angry. To be treated in this way while they were saving the people from the Indian knife and tomahawk was too bad. They marched against Jamestown again. This time the governor did not run away, but prepared to defend the place with soldiers and cannon.

But they did not fire their guns. Bacon had captured some of the wives of the principal men, and he put them in front of his line as he advanced. The governor did not dare bid his soldiers to fire on these women, so he left the town again in a hurry, and it was taken by the Indian fighters.

Bacon made up his mind that Governor Berkeley should not come back to Jamestown again. He had the town set on fire and burned to the ground. Some of the men with him set fire to their own houses, so that they should not give shelter to the governor and his men. That was the end of Jamestown. It was never rebuilt. Only ashes remained of the first English town in America. To-day there is only an old church tower to show where it stood.

We cannot tell what might have happened if brave young Bacon had lived. As it was, he was taken sick and died. His men now had no leader, and soon scattered. Then the governor came back full of fury, and began to hang all those who opposed him. He might have put a great many of them to death if the king had not stopped him and ordered him back to England. This was King Charles II., whose father had been put to death by Cromwell. He was angry at what Governor Berkeley had done, and said:

"That old fool has hung more men in that naked land than I did for the murder of my father."

CHAPTER VIII

OLD TIMES IN THE COLONIES

WHAT a wonderful change has come over this great country of ours since the days of our grandfathers! Look at our great cities, with their grand buildings, and their miles of streets, with swift-speeding electric cars, and thousands of carriages and wagons, and great stores lit by brilliant electric lights, and huge workshops filled with rattling wheels and marvelous machines! And look at our broad fields filled with cattle or covered by growing crops, and divided by splendid highways and railroads thousands of miles in length! Is it not all very wonderful?

"But has it not always been this way?" some very young persons ask. "I have lived so many years and have never seen anything else."

My dear young friend, if you had lived fifty or sixty years, as many of us older folks have, you would have seen very different things. And if we had lived as long ago as our grandfathers did, and then come back again to-day, I fancy our eyes would open wider than Governor Andros's did when he saw that the charter was gone.

In those days, as I told you, when any one wanted to make a light, he could not strike a match and touch it to a gas jet as we do, but must hammer away with flint and steel, and then had nothing better than a home-made tallow candle to light. Why, I am sure that many of you never even saw a pair of snuffers, which people then used to cut off the candle wick.

Some of you who live in old houses with dusty lofts under the roof, full of worm-eaten old furniture, have, no doubt, found there odd-looking wooden frames and wheels, and queer old tools of various kinds. Sometimes these wheels are brought down stairs and set in the hall as something to be proud of. And the old eight-day clocks stand there, too, with their loud "tick-tack," buzzing and ticking away to-day as if they had not done so for a hundred years. The wheels I speak of are the old spinning wheels, with which our great-grandmothers spun flax into thread. This thread they wove into homespun cloth on old-fashioned looms. All work of this kind used to be done at home, though now it is done in great factories; and we buy our clothes in the stores, instead of spinning and weaving and sewing them in the great old kitchens before the wood-fire on the hearth.

Really, I am afraid many of you do not know how people lived in the old times. They are often spoken of as the "good old times." I fancy you will hardly think so when I have told you something more about them. Would you think it very good to have to get up in a freezing cold room, and go down and pump ice-cold water to wash your face, and go out in the snow to get wood to make the fire, and shiver for an hour before the house began to warm up? That is only one of the things you would not find pleasant. I shall certainly have to stop here and tell you about how people lived in old times, and then you can say if you would like to go back to them.

Would any boy and girl among you care to live in a little one-story house, made of rough logs laid one on another, and with a roof of thatch—that is, of straw or reeds, or anything that would keep out the rain? Houses, I mean, with only one or two rooms, and some of them with chimneys made of wood, plastered with clay on the inside so that they could not be set on fire. These were the oldest houses. Later on people began to build larger houses, many of which were made of brick or stone. But I am afraid there was not much comfort in the best of them. They had no stoves, and were heated by great stone fireplaces, where big logs of wood were burned. They made a bright and cheerful blaze, it is true, but most of the heat went roaring up the wide chimney, and only a little of it got out into the room. In the winter the people lived in their kitchens, with the blazing wood-fire for heat and light, and at bed-time went shivering off to ice-cold rooms. Do you think you would have enjoyed that?

They had very little furniture, and the most of what they had was rude and rough, much of it chopped out of the trees by the farmer's axe. Some of the houses had glass windows—little diamond-shaped panes, set in lead frames—but most of them had nothing but oiled paper, which kept out as much light as it let in.

All the cooking was done on the great kitchen hearth, where the pots were hung on iron cranes and the pans set on the blazing coals. They did not have as many kinds of food to cook as we have. Mush and milk, or pork and beans, were their usual food, and their bread was mostly made of rye or cornmeal. The boys and girls who had nice books they wanted to read often had to do so by the light of the kitchen fire; but I can tell you that books were very scarce things in those days.

If any of us had lived then I know how glad we would have been to see the bright spring time, with its flowers and warm sunshine. But we might have shivered again when we thought of next winter. Of course, the people had some good times. They had Thanksgiving-day, when the table was filled with good things to eat, and election-day and training-day, when they had outdoor sports. And they had quilting and husking-parties, and spinning bees, and sleigh-rides and picnics and other amusements. A wedding was a happy time, and even a funeral was followed by a great dinner. But after all there was much more hard work than holiday, and nearly everybody had to labor long and got little for it. They were making themselves homes and a country, you know, and it was a very severe task. We, to-day, are getting the good of their work.

Down South people had more comfort. The weather was not nearly so cold, so they did not have to keep up such blazing fires or shiver in their cold beds. Many of the rich planters built themselves large mansions of wood or brick, and brought costly furniture from England, and lived in great show, with gold and silverware on their sideboards and fine coaches drawn by handsome horses when they went abroad.

In New York the Dutch built quaint old houses, of the kind used in Holland. In Philadelphia the Quakers lived in neat two-storied houses, with wide orchards and gardens round them, where they raised plenty of fruit. When any one opened a shop, he would hang out a basket, a wooden anchor, or some such sign to show what kind of goods he had to sell.

In New England Sunday was kept in a very strict fashion, for the people were very religious. It was thought wicked to play, or even to laugh, on Sunday, and everybody had to go to church. All who did not go were punished. And, mercy on us, what sermons they preached in those cold old churches, prosing away sometimes for two hours at a time! The boys and girls had to listen to them, as well as the men and women, and you know how hard it is now to listen for one hour.

If they got sleepy, as no doubt they often did, and went off into a snooze, they were soon wide awake again. For the constable went up and down the aisles with a long staff in his hand. This had a rabbit's foot on one end of it and a rabbit's tail on the other. If he saw one of the women asleep he would draw the rabbit's tail over her face. But if a boy took a nap, down would come the rabbit's foot in a sharp rap on his head, and up he would start very wide awake. To-day we would call that sort of sermons cruelty to children, and I think it was cruelty to the old folks also.

Do you think those were "good old times"? I imagine some of you will fancy they were "bad old times." But they were not nearly so bad as you may think. For you must bear in mind that the people knew nothing of many of the things we enjoy. They were used to hard work and plain food and coarse furniture and rough clothes and cold rooms, and were more hardy and could stand more than people who sleep in furnace-heated rooms and have their tables heaped with all kinds of fruits and vegetables and meats.

But there was one thing that could not have been pleasant, and that was, their being afraid all the time of the Indians, and having to carry muskets with them even when they went to church. All around them were the forests in which the wild red men roamed, and their cruel yell might be heard at any time, or a sharp arrow might whiz out from the thick leaves.

The farm-houses were built like forts, and in all the villages were strong buildings called blockhouses, to which everybody could run in times of danger. In these the second story spread out over the first, and there were holes in the floor through which the men could fire down on the Indians below. But it makes us tremble to think that, at any time, the traveler or farmer might be shot down by a lurking savage, or might be seized and burned alive. We can hardly wonder that the people grew to hate the Indians and to kill them or drive them away.

There was much game in the woods and the rivers were full of fish, so that many of the people spent their time in hunting and fishing. They got to be as expert in this as the Indians themselves, and some of them could follow a trail as well as the most sharp-sighted of the red men.

Some of you may have read Fenimore Cooper's novels of Indian life, and know what a wonderful hunter and Indian trailer old Natty Bumppo was. But we do not need to go to novels to read about great hunters, for the life of Daniel Boone is as full of adventure as that of any of the heroes of Indian life.

Daniel Boone was the most famous hunter this country has ever known. He lived much later than the early times I am talking about, but the country he lived in was as wild as that found by the first settlers of the country. When he was only a little boy he went into the deep woods and lived there by himself for several days, shooting game and making a fire to cook it by. He made himself a little hut of boughs and sods, and lived in it like an Indian, and there his father and friends found him when they came seeking him in the woods.

Years afterwards he crossed the high mountains of North Carolina and went into the great forest of Kentucky, where only Indians and wild animals lived. For a long time he stayed there by himself, with the Indians hunting and trying to kill him. But he was too wide awake for the smartest of them all.

One time, when they were close on his trail, he got away from them by catching hold of a loose grape-vine and making a long swinging jump, and then running on. When the Indians came to the place they lost the marks of his footprints and gave up the chase. At another time when he was taken prisoner he got up, took one of their guns, and slipped away from them without one of them waking up.

Many years afterwards, when he and others had built a fort in Kentucky, and brought out their wives and children, Boone's daughters and two other girls were carried off by Indians while they were out picking wild flowers.

Boone and other hunters were soon on their trail, and followed it by the broken bushes and bits of torn dress which the wide-awake young girls had left behind them. In this way they came up to the Indians while they were eating their supper, fired on them, and then ran up and rescued the girls. These young folks did not go out of the fort to pick wild flowers after that.

Once Daniel Boone was taken prisoner, and would have been burned alive if an old woman had not taken him for her son. The Indians painted his face and made him wear an Indian dress and live with them as one of themselves. But one day he heard them talking, and found that they were going to attack the fort where all his friendswere. Then he slipped out of the village and ran away. He had a long journey to make and the Indians followed him close. But he walked in the water to hide his footsteps, and lived on roots and berries, for fear they would hear his gun if he shot any game. In the end he got back safe to the fort. He found it in bad condition, but he set the men at work to make it strong, and when the Indians came they were beaten off.

Daniel Boone lived to be a very old man, and kept going farther west to get away from the new people who were coming into the Kentucky forest. He said he wanted "elbow room." He spent all the rest of his life hunting, and the Indians looked on him as the greatest woodsman and the most wonderful hunter the white men ever had.

CHAPTER IX

A HERO OF THE COLONIES

DO you not think there are a great many interesting stories in American history? I have told you some, and I could tell you many more. I am going to tell you one now, about a brave young man who had a great deal to do with the making of our glorious country. But to reach it we will have to take a step backward over one hundred and fifty years. That is a pretty long step, isn't it? It takes us away back to about the year 1750. But people had been coming into this country for more than a hundred and fifty years before that, and there were a great many white men and women in America at that time.

These people came from Spain and France and Great Britain and Holland and Germany and Sweden and other countries besides. The Spaniards had spread through many regions in the south; the French had gone west by way of the Great Lakes and then down the Mississippi River; but the British were settled close to the ocean, and the country back of them was still forest land, where only wild men and wild beasts lived. Thatis the way things were situated at the time of the story which I now propose to tell.

The young man I am about to speak of knew almost as much about life in the deep woods as Daniel Boone, the great hunter, of whom I have just told you. Why, when he was only sixteen years old he and another boy went far back into the wild country of Virginia to survey or measure the lands there for a rich land-holder.

The two boys crossed the rough mountains and went into the broad valley of the Shenandoah River, and for months they lived there alone in the broad forest. There were no roads through the woods and they had to make their own paths. When they were hungry they would shoot a wild turkey or a squirrel, or sometimes a deer. They would cook their meat by holding it on a stick over a fire of fallen twigs, and for plates they would cut large chips from a tree with their axe.

All day long they worked in the woods, measuring the land with a long chain. At night they would roll themselves in their blankets and go to sleep under the trees. If the weather was cold they gathered wood and made a fire. Very likely they enjoyed it all, for boys are fond of adventure. Sometimes a party of Indians would come up and be very curious to know what these white boys were doing. But the Indians were peaceful then,and did not try to harm them. One party amused the young surveyors by dancing a war dance before them. A fine time they had in the woods, where they stayed alone for months. When they came back the land-holder was much pleased with their work.

Now let us go on for five years, when the backwoods boy-surveyor had become a young man twenty-one years of age. If we could take ourselves back to the year 1753, and plunge into the woods of western Pennsylvania, we might see this young man again in the deep forest, walking along with his rifle in hand and his pack on his back. He had with him an old frontiersman named Gill, and an Indian who acted as their guide through the forest.

The Indian was a treacherous fellow. One day, when they were not looking, he fired his gun at them from behind a tree. He did not hit either of them. Some men would have shot him, but they did not; they let him go away and walked on alone through the deep woods. They built a fire that night, but they did not sleep before it, for they were afraid the Indian might come back and try to kill them while they were sleeping. So they left it burning and walked on a few miles and went to sleep without a fire.

A few days after that they came to the banks of a wide river. You may find it on your map of Pennsylvania. It is called the Allegheny River, and runs into the Ohio. It had been frozen, for it was winter time; but now the ice was broken and floating swiftly down the stream.

What were they to do? They had to get across that stream. The only plan they could think of was to build a raft out of logs and try to push it through the ice with long poles. This they did, and were soon out on the wild river and among the floating ice.

It was a terrible passage. The great cakes of ice came swirling along and striking like heavy hammers against the raft, almost hard enough to knock it to pieces. One of these heavy ice cakes struck the pole of the young traveler, and gave him such a shock that he fell from the raft into the freezing cold water. He had a hard enough scramble to get back on the raft again.

After a while they reached a little island in the stream and got ashore. There was no wood on it and they could not make a fire, so they had to walk about all night to keep from freezing. The young man was wet to the skin, but he had young blood and did not suffer as much as the older man with him. When morning came they found that the ice was frozen fast between the island and the other shore, so all they had to do was to walk across it.

These were not the only adventures they had, but they got safe back to Virginia, from which they had set out months before.

Do you want to know who this young traveler was? His name was George Washington. That is all I need say. Any one who does not know who George Washington was is not much of an American. But quite likely you do not guess what he was doing in the woods so far away from his home. He had been sent there by the governor of Virginia, and I shall have to tell you why.

But first you must go back with me to an earlier time. The time I mean is when the French were settling in Canada along the St. Lawrence River, and going west over the lakes, and floating in canoes down the Mississippi River to the Gulf of Mexico. Wherever they went they built forts and claimed the country for their king. At the same time the English were settling along the Atlantic shores and pushing slowly back into the country.

You should know that the French and the English were not the best of friends. They had their wars in Europe, and every time they got into war there they began to fight in America also. This made terrible times in the new country. The French had many of the Indians on their side, and they marched through the woods and attacked some of the English towns, and the cruel Indians murdered many of the poor settlers who had donethem no harm. There were three such wars, lasting for many years, and a great many innocent men, women and children, who had nothing to do with the wars in Europe, lost their lives. That is what we call war. It is bad enough now, but it was worse still in those days.

The greatest of all the wars between the French and the English was still to come. Between the French forts on the Mississippi and the English settlements on the Atlantic there was a vast forest land, and both the French and the English said it belonged to them. In fact, it did not belong to either of them, but to the Indians; but the white men never troubled themselves about the rights of the old owners of the land.

While the English were talking the French were acting. About 1750 they built two or three forts in the country south of Lake Erie. What they wanted was the Ohio River, with the rich and fertile lands which lay along that stream. Building those forts was the first step. The next step would be to send soldiers to the Ohio and build forts there also.

When the English heard what the French were doing they became greatly alarmed. If they did not do something very quickly they would lose all this great western country. The governor of Virginia wished to know what the French meant to do, and he thought the best way to find out was to askthem. So he chose the young backwoods surveyor, George Washington, and sent him through the great forest to the French forts.

Washington was very young for so important a duty. But he was tall and strong and quick-witted, and he was not afraid of any man or anything. And he knew all about life in the woods. So he was chosen, and far west he went over plain and mountain, now on horseback and now on foot, following the Indian trails through the forest, until at last he came to the French forts.

The French officers told him that they had come there to stay. They were not going to give up their forts to please the governor of Virginia. And Washington's quick eye saw that they were getting canoes ready to go down the streams to the Ohio River the next spring. This was the news the young messenger was taking back to the governor when he had his adventures with the Indian and the ice.

If any of you know anything about how wars are brought on, you may well think there was soon going to be war in America. Both parties wanted the land, and both were ready to fight to get it, and when people feel that way fighting is not far off.

Indeed, the spring of 1754 was not far advanced before both sides were on the move. Washington had picked out a beautiful spot for a fort. Thiswas where the two rivers which form the Ohio come together. On that spot the city of Pittsburg now stands; but then it was a very wild place.

As soon as the governor heard Washington's report he sent a party of men in great haste to build a fort at that point. But in a short time a larger party of French came down the Allegheny River in canoes and drove the English workmen away. Then they finished the fort for themselves and called it Fort Duquesne.

Meanwhile Washington was on his way back. A force of four hundred Virginians had been sent out under an officer named Colonel Frye. But the colonel died on the march, and young Washington, then only twenty-two years old, found himself at the head of a regiment of soldiers, and about to start a great war. Was it not a difficult position for so young a man? Not many men of that age would have known what to do, but George Washington was not an ordinary man.

While the Virginians were marching west, the French were marching south, and it was not long before they came together. A party of French hid in a thicket to watch the English, and Washington, thinking they were there for no good, ordered his men to fire. They did so, and the leader of the French was killed. This was the first shot in the coming war.

But the youthful commander soon found thatthe French were too strong for him. He built a sort of fort at a place called Great Meadows, and named it Fort Necessity. It was hardly finished before the French and Indians came swarming all around it and a severe fight began.

The Virginians fought well, but the French were too strong, and fired into the fort till Washington had to surrender. This took place on July 4, 1754, just twenty-two years before the American Declaration of Independence. Washington and his men were allowed to march home with their arms, and the young colonel was very much praised when he got home, for everybody thought he had done his work in the best possible way.

When the news of this battle crossed the ocean there was great excitement in England and France, and both countries sent soldiers to America. Those from England were under a general named Braddock, a man who knew all about fighting in England, but knew nothing about fighting in America. And what was worse, he would let nobody tell him. Washington generously tried to do so, but he got snubbed by the proud British general for his pains.

After a while away marched General Braddock, with his British soldiers in their fine red coats. Washington went with him with a body of Virginians dressed in plain colony clothes. On and on they went, through the woods and over themountains, cutting down trees and opening a road for their wagons, and bravely beating their drums and waving their flags. At length they came near Fort Duquesne, the drums still beating, the flags still flying, the gun barrels glittering in the bright sunshine.

"Let me go ahead with my Virginians," said Washington. "They know all about Indian fighting."

"That for your Indians!" said Braddock, snapping his fingers. "They will not stay in their hiding places long when my men come up."

Soon after they came into a narrow place, with steep banks and thick bushes all around. And suddenly loud Indian war-whoops and the crack of guns came from those bushes. Not a man could be seen, but bullets flew like hail-stones among the red-coats. The soldiers fired back, but they wasted their bullets on the bushes. Washington and his men ran into the woods and got behind trees like the Indians, but Braddock would not let his men do the same, and they were shot down like sheep. At length General Braddock fell wounded, and then his brave red-coats turned and ran for their lives. Very likely not a man of them would have got away if Washington and his men had not kept back the French and Indians.

This defeat was a bad business for the poor settlers,for the savage redskins began murdering them on all sides, and during all the rest of the war Washington was kept busy fighting with these Indians. Not till four years afterwards was he able to take Fort Duquesne from the French.

Then another body of men was sent through the woods and over the mountains to capture this fort. But their general did as Braddock had done before him, spending so much time cutting a highroad through the woods that the whole season passed away and he was ready to turn and march back. Then Washington, who was with him, asked permission to go forward with his rangers. The general told him to go and he hurried through the woods and to the fort. When he came near it the French took to their boats and paddled off down the river, so that Washington took the fort without firing a shot.

CHAPTER X

THE FRENCH AND INDIAN WAR AND THE STORY OF THE ACADIANS

HAVE any of my young readers read the beautiful poem of "Evangeline," written by the poet Longfellow? Very likely it is too old for you, though the time will come when you will read it and enjoy it greatly. Evangeline was a pretty and pious woman who lived in a French settlement called Acadia, on the Atlantic coast. You will not find this name on any of your maps, but must look for Nova Scotia, by which name Acadia is now known. The story of Evangeline tells us about the cruel way in which the poor Acadians were treated by the English. It is a sad and pathetic story, as you will see when you have read it.

It was one of the wicked results of the war between the French and the English. There were many cruel deeds in this war, and the people who suffered the most were those who had the least to do with the fighting. In one place a quiet, happy family of father, mother and children, living on a lonely farm, and not dreaming of anydanger, suddenly hear the wild war-whoop of the Indians, and soon see their doors broken open and their house blazing, and are carried off into cruel captivity—those who are not killed on the spot. In another place all the people of a village are driven from their comfortable homes by soldiers and forced to wander and beg their bread in distant lands. And all this takes place because the kings of England and France, three thousand miles away, are quarreling about some lands which do not belong to either of them. If those who brought on wars had to suffer for them they would soon come to an end. But they revel and feast in their splendid palaces while poor and innocent people endure the suffering. The war that began in the wilds of western Pennsylvania, between the French and Indians and the English lasted seven years, from 1754 to 1761. During that time there were many terrible battles, and thousands of soldiers were killed, and there was much suffering and slaughter among the people, and burning of houses, and destruction of property, and horrors of all sorts.

It is called the French and Indian War, because there were many Indians on the side of the French. There were some on the side of the English, also. Indians are very savage and cruel in their way of fighting, as you already know. I shall have to tell you one instance of their love of bloodshed.One of the English forts, called Fort William Henry, which stood at the southern end of Lake George, had to surrender to the French, and its soldiers were obliged to march out and give up their guns.

There were a great many Indians with the French, and while the prisoners stood outside the fort, without a gun in their hands, the savage men attacked them and began to kill them with knives and tomahawks. The French had promised to protect them, but they stood by and did nothing to stop this terrible slaughter, and many of the helpless soldiers were murdered. Others were carried off by the Indians as prisoners. It was the most dreadful event of the whole cruel war.

I must now ask you to look on a map of the State of New York, if you have any. There you will find the Hudson River, and follow it up north from the city of New York, past Albany, the capital of the state, until it ends in a region of mountains. Near its upper waters is a long, narrow lake named Lake George, which is full of beautiful islands. North of that is a much larger lake named Lake Champlain, which reaches up nearly to Canada.

The British had forts on the Hudson River and Lake George and the French on Lake Champlain, and also between the two lakes, where stood the strong Fort Ticonderoga. It was around theseforts and along these lakes that most of the fighting took place. For a long time the French had the best of it. The British lost many battles and were driven back. But they had the most soldiers, and in the end they began to defeat the French and drive them back, and Canada became the seat of war. But let me tell you the story of the Acadians.

Acadia was a country which had been settled by the French a long, long time before, away back in 1604, before there was an English settlement in America. Captain John Smith, you know, came to America in 1607, three years afterwards. Acadia was a very fertile country, and the settlers planted fields of grain and orchards of apples and other fruits, and lived a very happy life, with neat houses and plenty of good food, and in time the whole country became a rich farming land.

But the British would not let these happy farmers alone. Every time there was trouble with the French, soldiers were sent to Acadia. It was captured by the British in 1690, but was given back to France in 1697, when that war ended. It was taken again by the British in the war that began in 1702, and this time it was not given back. Even its name of Acadia was taken away, and it was called Nova Scotia, which is not nearly so pretty a name.

Thus it was that, when the new war withFrance began, Acadia was held as a province of Great Britain. To be sure the most of its people were descended from the old French settlers and did not like their British masters, but they could not help themselves, and went on farming in their old fashion. They were ignorant, simple-minded countrymen, who looked upon France as their country, and were not willing to be British subjects.

That is the way with the French. It is the same to-day in Canada, which has been a colony of Great Britain for nearly a century and a half. The descendants of the former French still speak their old language and love their old country, and now sometimes fight the British with their votes as they once did with their swords.

The British did not hold the whole of Acadia. The country now called New Brunswick, which lies north of Nova Scotia, was part of it, and was still held by the French. In 1755 the British government decided to attempt the capture of this country, and sent out soldiers for that purpose. Fighting began, but the French defended themselves bravely, and the British found they had a hard task to perform.

What made it worse for them was that some of the Acadians, who did not want to see the British succeed, acted as spies upon them, and told the French soldiers about their movements, so thatthe French were everywhere ready for them. And the Acadians helped the French in other ways, and gave the British a great deal of trouble.

This may have been wrong, but it was natural. Every one feels like helping his friends against his enemies. But you may be sure that it made the British very angry, and in the end they took a cruel resolution. This was to send all the Acadians away from their native land to far-off, foreign countries. It was not easy to tell who were acting as spies, so the English government ordered them all to be removed. They were told they might stay if they would swear to be true subjects of the king of England, but this the most of them would not do, for they were French at heart, and looked on King Louis of France as their true and rightful ruler.

Was not this very cruel? There were hundreds of boys and girls like yourselves among these poor Acadians, who had happy homes, and loved to work and play in their pretty gardens and green fields, and whose fathers and mothers did no harm to any one. But because a few busy men gave news to the French, all of these were to be torn from their comfortable homes and sent far away to wander in strange lands, where many of them would have to beg for bread. It was a heartless act, and the world has ever since said so, and among all the cruel things the British have done,the removal of the Acadians from their homes is looked upon as one of the worst.

When soldiers are sent to do a cruel thing they are very apt to do it in the most brutal fashion. The Acadians did not know what was to be done. It was kept secret for fear they might run away and hide. A large number of soldiers were sent out, and they spread like a net over a wide stretch of country. Then they marched together and drove the people before them. The poor farmers might be at their dinners or working in their fields, but they were told that they must stop everything and leave their homes at once, for they were to be sent out of the country. Just think of it! What a grief and terror they must have been in!

They were hardly given time to gather the few things they could carry with them, and on all sides they were driven like so many sheep to the seaside town of Annapolis, to which ships had been brought to carry them away. More than six thousand of these unhappy people, old and young, men, women and little ones, were gathered there; many of them weeping bitterly, many more with looks of despair on their faces, all of them sad at heart and very likely wishing they were dead.

Around them were soldiers to keep them from running away. They were made to get on the ships in such haste that families were often separated, husband and wife, or children and theirmothers, being put on different ships and sent to different places. And for fear that some of them might come back again their houses were burned and their farms laid waste. Many of them went to the French settlements in Louisiana, and others to other parts of America. Poor exiles! they were scattered widely over the earth. Some of them in time came back to their loved Acadia, but the most of them never saw it again. It was this dreadful act about which Longfellow wrote in his poem of Evangeline.

Now I must tell you how the French and Indian War ended. The French had two important cities in Canada, Montreal and Quebec. Quebec was built on a high and steep hill and was surrounded by strong walls, behind which were more than eight thousand soldiers. It was not an easy city to capture.

A large British fleet was sent against it, and also an army of eight thousand men, under General Wolfe. For two or three months they fired at the city from the river below, but the French scorned them from their steep hilltop. At length General Wolfe was told of a narrow path by which he might climb the hill. One dark night he tried it, and by daybreak a large body of men had reached the hill-top, and had dragged up a number of cannon with them.

When the French saw this they were frightened.They hurried out of the city, thinking they could drive the English over the precipice before any more of them got up. They were mistaken in this. The English met them boldly, and in the battle that followed they gained the victory and Quebec fell into their hands.

General Wolfe was mortally wounded, but when he was told that the French were in flight, he said: "God be praised! I die happy."

Montcalm, the French general, also fell wounded. When he knew that he must die he said: "So much the better; I shall not live to see the surrender of Quebec."

The next year Montreal was taken, and the war ended. And in the treaty of peace France gave up all her colonies in America. England got Canada and Spain got Louisiana. All North America now belonged to two nations, England and Spain.

CHAPTER XI

THE CAUSES OF THE REVOLUTION

I SHOULD be glad to have some of you take a steamboat ride up the broad Hudson River, past the city of New York, and onward in the track of the "Half Moon," Henry Hudson's ship. If you did so, you would come in time to the point where this ship stopped and turned back. Here, where Hudson and his Dutch sailors saw only a great spread of forest trees, stretching far back from the river bank, our modern travelers would see the large and handsome city of Albany, the capital of the State of New York.

This is one of the hundreds of fine cities which have grown up in our country since Henry Hudson's time. A hundred and fifty years ago it was a small place, not much larger than many of our villages. But even then it was of importance, for in it was taken the first step towards our great Union of States. I shall have to tell you what this step was, for you will certainly want to know.

Well, at the time I speak of there was no such thing as an American Union. There were thirteencolonies, reaching from New Hampshire down to Georgia. But each of these was like a little nation of its own; each had its own government, made its own laws, and fought its own fights. This was well enough in one way, but it was not so well in another. At one time the people had the Indians to fight with, at another time the French, and sometimes both of these together, and many of them thought that they could do their fighting better if they were united into one country.

So in the year 1754 the colonies sent some of their best men to Albany, to talk over this matter, and see if a union of the colonies could not be made. This is what I meant when I said that the first step towards the American Union was taken at Albany.

Of these men, there is only one I shall say anything about. This man's name you should know and remember, for he was one of the noblest and wisest men that ever lived in this country. His name was Benjamin Franklin. Forty years before this time he was a little Boston boy at work in his father's shop, helping him make candles. Afterwards he learned how to print, and then, in 1723, he went to Philadelphia, where he soon had a shop and a newspaper office, and in time became rich.

There was nothing going on that Franklin didnt take part in. In his shop he bound books, he made ink, he sold rags, soap, and coffee. He was not ashamed of honest work, and would take off his coat and wheel his papers along the street in a wheelbarrow. He started many institutions in Philadelphia which are now very important. Among these there are a great university, a large hospital, and a fine library. No doubt you have read how he brought down the lightning from the clouds along the string of a kite, and proved that lightning is the same thing as electricity. And he took an active part in all the political movements of the time. That is why he came to be sent to Albany in 1754, as a member of the Albany Convention.

Franklin always did things in ways that set people to thinking. When he went to Albany he took with him copies of a queer picture which he had printed in his newspaper. This was a snake cut into thirteen pieces. Under each piece was the first letter of the name of a colony, such as "P" for Pennsylvania. Beneath the whole were the words "Unite or die."

That was like Franklin; he was always doing something odd. The cut-up snake stood for the thirteen divided colonies. What Franklin meant was that they could not exist alone. A snake is not of much account when it is chopped up into bits, but it is a dangerous creature when it is whole.He proposed that there should be a grand council of all the colonies, a sort of Congress, meeting every year in Philadelphia, which was the most central large city. Over them all was to be a governor-general appointed by the king. This council could make laws, lay taxes, and perform other important duties.

That is enough to say about Franklin's plan, for it was not accepted. It was passed by the convention, it is true, but the king would not have it and the colonies did not want it; so the snake still lay stretched out along the Atlantic in thirteen pieces. Then came the great war with the French of which I have told you. After that was over, things came to pass which in the end forced the colonies to combine. Thus Franklin's plan, or something like it, was in time carried out, but for many years the country was in a terrible state. This is what I am now going to tell you about.

You should know that the war with the French cost the king and the colonies a great deal of money. The king of England at that time was named George. He was an obstinate man, but not a very wise one, as you will think when you have learned more about him. One thing he wanted to do was to send soldiers to America to keep the French from getting back what they had lost, and he asked the people to pay these soldiers. He also asked them to send him money to paythe governors and judges whom he had chosen to rule over them. But the people thought they could take care of themselves, and did not want British soldiers. And they preferred to pay the governors and judges themselves as they had always done, and did not want King George to do it for them. So they would not send him the money he asked for.

Some of you may think this was very mean in the Americans, after all the British had done to help them in their war with the French. But they knew very well what they were about. They thought that if they gave the king a dollar to-day he might want five dollars to-morrow, and ten dollars the next day. They judged it best not to begin with the dollar. Kings, you should know, do not always make the best use of money that is given them by their people.

And that was not all. The people in the colonies did not like the way they had been treated by the English. They had mountains full of iron, but the king would not let them make this iron into tools. They had plenty of wool, but he would not let them weave it into cloth. They must buy these and other things in England, and must keep at farming; but they were not allowed to send their grain to England, but had to eat it all at home. They could not even send goods from one colony to another. Thus they were to be keptpoor that the rich English merchants and manufacturers might grow rich.

These were some of the things the American people had to complain of. There were still other things, and a good many of the Americans had very little love for the English king and people. They felt that they were in a sort of slavery, and almost as if they had ropes on their hands and chains on their feet.

When King George was told that the Americans would not send him money he was very angry. I am afraid he called them bad names. They were a low, ignorant, ungrateful set, he said, and he would show them who was their master. He would tax them and get money from them in that way. So the English Parliament, which is a body of lawmakers like our Congress, came together and passed laws to tax the Americans.

The first tax they laid is what is called a stamp tax. I fancy you know very well what that is, for we have had a stamp tax in this country more than once, when the government was in need of money. Everybody who wrote a bank check, or made any legal paper, or sent away an express package, had to buy a stamp from the government and put it on the paper; and stamps had to be used on many other things.

But there is this difference. Our people were quite willing to buy these stamps, but they werenot willing to buy the stamps which the British government sent them in 1765. Why? Well, they had a good reason for it, and this was that they had nothing to do with making the law. The English would not pay any taxes except those made by the people whom they elected to Parliament, and the Americans said they had the same right. They were not allowed to send any members to Parliament, so they said that Parliament had no right to tax them. Their own legislatures might vote to send the king money, but the English Parliament had no right to vote for them.

When the king found that the Americans would not use his stamps he tried another plan. He laid a tax on tea and some other goods. He thought that our people could not do without tea, so he sent several shiploads across the ocean, expecting them to buy it and pay the tax. But he soon found that the colonists had no more use for taxed tea than for stamps. They would not even let the captains bring their tea on shore, except at Charleston, and there it was packed in damp cellars, where it soon rotted. A ship sent to Annapolis was set on fire and burned to the water's edge with the tea in it.

But the most stirring event took place at Boston. There one night, while the tea-ship lay at a wharf in the harbor, a number of young men dressed like Indians rushed on board with a loudwar-whoop and began to break open the tea-chests with their hatchets and pour the tea into the harbor. This was the famous "Boston tea-party."

Americans liked tea, but not tea with an English tax on it. They boiled leaves and roots and made some sort of tea out of them. It was poor stuff, but they did not pay any tax. And they would not buy any cloth or other goods brought from England. If the king was angry and stubborn they were angry and stubborn, too, and every day they grew more angry, until many of them began to think that they would be better off without a king. They were not the kind of people to be made slaves of easily by King George or any other king.

When the king heard of the "Boston tea-party" he was in a fury. He would make Boston pay well for its tea, he said. So he sent soldiers there, and he gave orders that no ships should go into or out of Boston harbor. This stopped most of the business of the town, and soon the poor people had no work to do and very little to eat. But they had crowded meetings at Faneuil Hall, where Samuel Adams and John Hancock and other patriots talked to them of their rights and wrongs. It began to look as if war would soon come.

The time had come at last for a union of the colonies. What Franklin had failed to do at Albany in 1754 was done at Philadelphia in 1774.A meeting was held there which was called a Congress, and was made up of some of the best men of the country sent from the colonies. One of these was George Washington, who had lived on his farm at Mount Vernon since the end of the French War.

Congress sent a letter to the king, asking him to give the people of this country the same rights that the people of England had. There was no harm in this, I am sure, but it made the king more obstinate still. I have said he was not a wise man. Most people say he was a very foolish one, or he would have known that the people of the colonies would fight for their rights if they could not get them in peace.

All around Boston the farmers and villagers began to collect guns and powder and to drill men into soldiers. These were called "minute men," which meant that they would be ready to fight at a minute's notice, if they were asked to. When people begin to get ready in this way, war is usually not far off.

One night at Boston a man named Paul Revere stood watching a distant steeple till he saw a light suddenly flash out through the darkness. Then he leaped on his horse and rode at full speed away. That light was a signal telling him that British soldiers were on the march to Concordtwenty miles away, to destroy some powder and guns which had been gathered there for the use of these "minute men."

Away rode Revere through the night, rousing up the people and shouting to them that the British soldiers were coming. He was far ahead of the soldiers, so that when they reached the village of Lexington, ten miles from Boston, the people were wide awake, and a party of minute men was drawn up on the village green. The soldiers were ordered to fire on these men, and some of them fell dead. Those were the first shots in a great war. It was the 19th of April, 1775.

The British marched on to Concord, but the farmers had carried away most of the stores and buried them in the woods. Then the red-coats started back, and a terrible march they had of it. For all along the road were farmers with guns in their hands, firing on the troops from behind trees and stone walls. Some of the soldiers got back to Boston, but many of them lay dead in the road. The poor fellows killed at Lexington were terribly avenged.

Far and wide spread the news, and on all sides the farmers left their plows and took down their rifles, and thousands of them set out along the roads to Boston. Soon there were twenty thousand armed men around the town, and the British were shut up like rats in a trap. The American people werein rebellion against the king and war had begun.

It was to be a long and dreadful war, but it led to American liberty, and that was a thing well worth fighting for. While the people were laying siege to Boston, Congress was in session at Philadelphia, talking about what had best be done. One good thing they did was to make George Washington commander-in-chief of the army and send him to Boston to fight the British there. They could not have found a better soldier in all America.

The next good thing took place a year later. This was the great event which you celebrate with fireworks every 4th of July. Congress decided that this country ought to be free, and no longer to be under the rule of an English king. So a paper was written by a member from Virginia named Thomas Jefferson, with the help of Benjamin Franklin and some others. The paper is known by the long name of "Declaration of Independence." It declared that the American colonies were free from British rule, and in future would take care of themselves. It was on the 4th of July, 1776, that this great paper was adopted by Congress, and on that day the Republic of the United States of America was born. That is why our people have such a glad and noisy time every 4th of July.

Everywhere the people were full of joy whenthey heard what had been done. In the state house at Philadelphia rang out the great bell on which the words, "Proclaim liberty throughout the land and to all the inhabitants thereof." In New York the statue of King George was pulled down and thrown into the dust of the street. The people did not know what dark days lay before them, but they were ready to suffer much for the sake of liberty, and to risk all they had, life and all, for the freedom of their native land.

CHAPTER XII

FIGHTING FOR FREEDOM

ANY of my readers who are true, sound-hearted Americans, and I am sure all of them are that, would have been glad to see how the New England farmers swarmed around Boston in April, 1775. Some of them had fought in the French War, and brought with them their old rusty muskets, which they knew very well how to use. And most of them were hunters and had learned how to shoot. And all of them were bold and brave and were determined to have a free country. The English red-coat soldiers in Boston would soon find that these countrymen were not men to be laughed at, even if they had not been trained in war.

One morning the English woke up and rubbed their eyes hard, for there, on a hill that overlooked the town, was a crowd of Americans. They had been at work all night, digging and making earthworks to fight behind, and now had quite a fort. The English officers did not like the look of things, for the Americans could fire from that hill—Bunker Hill, they called it— straight downinto the town. They must be driven away or they would drive the troops away.

I can tell you that was a busy and bloody day for Boston. The great war-ships in the harbor thundered with their cannon at the men on the hill. And the soldiers began to march up the hill, thinking that the Yankees would run like sheep when they saw the red-coats coming near. But the Yankees were not there to run.

"Don't fire, boys, till you see the whites of their eyes," said brave General Prescott.

So the Yankee boys waited till the British were close at hand. Then they fired and the red-coats fell in rows, for the farmers did not waste their bullets. Those that did not fall scampered in haste down the hill. It was a strange sight to see British soldiers running away from Yankee farmers.

After a while the British came again. They were not so sure this time. Again the Yankee muskets rattled along the earthworks, and again the British turned and ran—those who were able to.

They could never have taken that hill if the farmer soldiers had not run out of powder. When the red-coats came a third time the Yankees could not fire, and had to fight them with the butts of their guns. So the British won the hill; butthey had found that the Yankee farmers were not cowards; after that time they never liked to march against American earthworks.

Not long after the battle of Bunker Hill General Washington came to command the Americans, and he spent months in drilling and making soldiers out of them. He also got a good supply of powder and muskets and some cannon, and one dark night in March, 1776, he built a fort on another hill that looked down on Boston.

I warrant you, the British were alarmed when they looked up that hill the next morning and saw cannon on its top and men behind the cannon. They would have to climb that hill as they had done Bunker Hill, or else leave Boston. But they had no fancy for another Bunker Hill, so they decided to leave. They went on board their ships and sailed away, and Washington and his men marched joyfully into the town. That was a great day for America, and it was soon followed by the 4th of July and the glorious Declaration of Independence. Since that 4th of July no king has ever ruled over the United States.

We call this war the American Revolution. Do you know what a revolution is? It means the doing away with a bad government and replacing it with a better one. In this country it meant that our people were tired of the rule of England andwished to govern themselves. They had to fight hard for their freedom, it is true, but it was well worth fighting for.

The war was a long and dreadful one. It went on for seven long years. At one time everything seemed lost; at other times all grew bright and hopeful. And thus it went on, up and down, to the end. I cannot tell you all that took place, but I will give you the important facts.

After the British left Boston, they sailed about for a time, and then they came with a large army to New York. Washington was there with his soldiers to meet them, and did his best, but everything seemed to go wrong. First, the Americans were beaten in battle and had to march out of New York and let the British march in. Then Washington and his ragged men were obliged to hasten across the State of New Jersey with a strong British force after them. They were too weak to face the British.

When they got to the Delaware River the Americans crossed it and took all the boats, so that the British could not follow them. It was now near winter time, and both armies went into winter quarters. They faced each other, but the wide river ran between.

You may well think that by this time the American people were getting very down-hearted. Many of them thought that all was lost, and thatthey would have to submit to King George. The army dwindled away and no new soldiers came in, so that it looked as if it would go to pieces. It was growing very dark for American liberty.

WASHINGTON CROSSING THE DELAWARE.

But there was one man who did not despair, and that man was George Washington. He saw that something must be done to stir up the spirits of the people, and he was just the man to do it. It was a wonderful Christmas he kept that year. All Christmas day his ragged and hungry soldiers were marching up their side of the Delaware, and crossing the river in boats, though the wind was biting cold, and the air was full of falling snow, and the broken ice was floating in great blocks down the river; but nothing stopped the gallant soldiers. All Christmas night they marched down the other side of the river, though their shoes were so bad that the ground became reddened by blood from their feet. Two of the poor fellows were frozen to death.

At Trenton, a number of miles below, there was a body of German soldiers. These had been hired by King George to help him fight his battles. That day they had been eating a good Christmas dinner while the hungry Americans were marching through the snow. At night they went to bed, not dreaming of danger.

They were wakened in the morning by shots and shouts. Washington and his men were in thestreets of the town. They had hardly time to seize their guns before the ragged Yankees were all around them and nearly all of them were made prisoners of war.

Was not that a great and glorious deed? It filled the Americans with new hope. In a few days afterwards, Washington defeated the British in another battle, and then settled down with his ragged but brave men in the hills of New Jersey. He did not go behind a river this time. The British knew where he was and could come to see him if they wanted to. But they did not come. Very likely they had seen enough of him for that winter.

The next year things went wrong again for Washington. A large British army sailed from New York and landed at the head of Chesapeake Bay. Then they marched overland to Philadelphia. Washington fought a battle with them on Brandywine Creek, but his men were defeated and the British marched on and entered Philadelphia. They now held the largest cities of the country, Philadelphia and New York.

While the British were living in plenty and having a very good time in the Quaker city, the poor Americans spent a wretched and terrible winter at a place called Valley Forge. The winter was a dismally cold one, and the men had not halfenough food to eat or clothes to wear, and very poor huts to live in. They suffered dreadfully, and before the spring came many of them died from disease and hardship.

Poor fellows! they were paying dearly for their struggle for liberty. But there was no such despair this winter as there had been the winter before, for news came from the north that warmed the soldiers up like a fire. Though Washington had lost a battle, a great victory had been gained by the Americans at Saratoga, in the upper part of New York state.

While General Howe was marching on Philadelphia, another British army, under General Burgoyne, had been marching south from Canada, along the line of Lake Champlain and Lake George. But Burgoyne and his men soon found themselves in a tight place. Food began to run short and a regiment of a thousand men was sent into Vermont to seize some stores. They were met by the Green Mountain boys, led by Colonel Stark, a brave old soldier.

"There are the red-coats," said the bold colonel. "We must beat them to-day, or Molly Stark is a widow."[1]

Beat them they did. Only seventy men got back to Burgoyne. All the rest were killed or captured.

Another force, under Colonel St. Leger, marched south from Oswego, on Lake Ontario. A large body of Indians was with him. This army stopped to besiege a fort in the wilderness, and General Arnold marched to help the fort.

The way Arnold defeated St. Leger was a very curious one. He sent a half-witted fellow into the Indian camp with the tale that a great American force was coming. The messenger came running in among the savages, with bullet-holes in his clothes. He seemed half scared to death, and told the Indians that a vast host was coming after him as thick as the leaves on the trees.

This story frightened the Indians and they ran off in great haste through the woods. When the British soldiers saw this they fell into such a terror that they took to their heels, leaving all their tents and cannon behind them. The people in the fort did not know what it meant, till Arnold came up and told them how he had won a victory without firing a shot, by a sort of fairy story.

All this was very bad for Burgoyne. The Indians he brought with him began to leave. At length he found himself in a terrible plight. His provisions were nearly gone, he was surrounded by the Americans, and after fighting two battleshe retreated to Saratoga. Here he had to surrender. He and all his army became prisoners to the Americans.

We cannot wonder that this warmed up the Americans like a fire. It filled the English with despair. They began to think that they would never win back the colonies.

One thing the good news did was to get the French to come to the help of the Americans. Benjamin Franklin was then in Paris, and he asked the king to send ships and men and money to America. The French had no love for the British, who had taken from them all their colonies in America, so they did as Franklin wished.

There are two more things I wish to tell you in this chapter, one good and one bad. When the British in Philadelphia heard that the French were coming to help the Americans, they were afraid they might be caught in a trap. So they left in great haste and marched for New York. Washington followed and fought a battle with them, but they got away. After that Washington's army laid siege to New York, as it had formerly done to Boston.

That was the good thing. The bad thing was this. General Benedict Arnold, who had defeated St. Leger and his Indians, and who was one of the bravest of the American officers, turned traitor to his country. He had charge of West Point, astrong fort on the Hudson River, and tried to give this up to the British. But he was found out and had to flee for his life. Major André, a British officer, who had been sent to talk with Arnold, was caught by three American scouts on his way back to New York. They searched him for papers, and found what they wanted hidden in his boot. Poor André was hung for a spy, but the traitor Arnold escaped. But he was hated by the Americans and despised by the British, and twenty years afterwards he died in shame and remorse.

FOOTNOTE:

[1] All the accounts agree that Colonel Stark spoke of his wife as "Molly Stark." But it has been found that his wife's name was Elizabeth; so he may have said "Betty Stark."

CHAPTER XIII

PAUL JONES, THE NAVAL HERO OF THE REVOLUTION

WE are justly proud of our great war-ships, with their strong steel sides and their mighty guns, each of which can hurl a cannon-ball miles and miles away. And such balls! Why, one of them is as heavy as a dozen of you tied together, and can bore a hole through a plate of solid steel as thick as your bodies.

Such ships and such guns as these had not been dreamed of in the days of the Revolution. Then there were only small wooden vessels, moved by sails instead of steam, and a cannon-ball that weighed twenty-four pounds was thought very heavy. Six and twelve-pound balls were common. And to hit a ship a mile away! It was not to be thought of. I tell you, in those days ships had to fight nearly side by side and men to fight face to face. To be a mile away was as good as being a hundred miles.

But for all this there was some hard fighting done at sea in the Revolutionary War, in spite of the small ships and little guns. They foughtcloser together, that was all. Boast as we may about the wonderful work done by our ships at Santiago and Manila in the Spanish War, we have better right to be proud of the deeds of our great naval hero of the Revolutionary War, with his rotten old ship and poor little guns, but with his stout heart behind them all.

This hero was the sturdy John Paul Jones, one of the boldest and bravest men that ever stood on a ship's deck. And his great sea fight has never been surpassed in all the history of naval war. I cannot tell you the story of the Revolution without telling about the great ocean victory of the bold-hearted Paul Jones.

Ships poor enough were those we had to fight with. A little fleet of seven or eight small vessels, whose heaviest guns threw only nine-pound balls, and the most of them only six-pound. You could have thrown these yourself with one hand, though not so far. These were all we had at first to fight more than seventy British ships, with guns that threw eighteen-pound balls, and some still heavier. Do you not think it looked like a one-sided fight?

But the Americans had one great advantage. They had not many merchant ships and not much to lose upon the seas. On the other hand, the ocean swarmed with the merchant ships of England, and with the store ships bringing supplies of guns and powder and food to the armies on shore. Herewere splendid prizes for our gallant seamen, and out of every port sailed bold privateers, or war-ships sent out by their owners, and not by the government, sweeping the seas and bringing in many a richly-laden craft.

Some of the best fighting of the war was done by these privateers. While they were hunting for merchant ships they often came across war-ships, and you can be sure they did not always run away. No, indeed; they were usually ready to fight, and during the war no less than sixteen war-vessels were captured by our ocean rovers. On the other hand, the British privateers did not capture a single American war-ship. As for merchant vessels, our privateers brought them in by the dozens. One fleet of sixty vessels set out from Ireland for the West Indies, and out of these thirty-five were gobbled up by our privateers, and their rich stores brought into American ports. During the whole war the privateers took more than seven hundred prizes. I might go on to tell you of some of their hard fights, but I think you would rather read the story of Paul Jones, the boldest and bravest of them all, the terror of the seas to the British fleet.

Paul Jones, you should know, was born in Scotland. But he made America his home. And as he was known to be a good sailor, he was appointed first lieutenant of the "Alfred," the flagship of our small fleet. He had the honor to be the first manto raise a flag on an American man-of-war, and that is something to be proud of. This took place on the "Delaware," at Philadelphia, about Christmas, 1775.

It was an important event for the fleet was just being sent out. At a given signal Lieutenant Jones grasped the halliards, and hauled up to the mizzen topmast a great flag of yellow silk. As it unfurled to the breeze cannon roared and crowds on the shore lustily cheered. In the centre of the flag was seen the figure of a green pine tree, and under this a rattlesnake lay coiled, with the warning motto, "Don't tread on me!"

This was the famous rattlesnake flag. Another flag was raised on which were thirteen stripes, in turns red and white, and in the corner the British union jack. We then had the stripes but not the stars. They were to come after the Declaration of Independence and the union of the states.

In August, 1776, Congress made Paul Jones captain of the brig "Providence," and he soon showed what kind of a man he was. He came across a fleet of five vessels, and made up his mind to capture the largest of them, which he thought to be a fine merchant ship. He got pretty close up before he learned his mistake. It was the British frigate "Solebay," strong enough to make mince-meat of his little brig. There was nothing for it but to run, and Captain Jones made hasteto get away, followed by the

"Solebay." But the Briton gained on the American, and after a four-hours' run the frigate was less than a hundred yards away. It might at any minute sink the daring little "Providence" by a broadside.

But Paul Jones was not the man to be caught. Suddenly the helm of the brig was put hard up, as sailors say, and the little craft turned and dashed across the frigate's bow. As it did so the flag of the republic was spread to the breeze, and a broadside from the brig's guns swept the frigate's deck. Then, with all sail set, away dashed the "Providence" before the breeze. As soon as the British got back their senses they fired all their guns at the brig. But not a ball hit her, and with the best of the wind she soon left the "Solebay" far behind.

And now I must tell the story of Paul Jones' greatest fight. In its way it was the greatest sea-fight ever known. It was fought with a fleet in which Jones sailed from a French port, for Congress had found what a hero they had in their Scotch sailor, and now they made him commodore of a fleet.

The flagship of this fleet was a rotten old log of a ship, which had sailed in the East India merchant service till its timbers were in a state of dry rot. It was a shapeless tub of a vessel, better fitted to lie in port and keep rabbits in than to sendout as a battle-ship. Paul Jones named it the "Bon Homme Richard," which, in English means "Poor Richard." This was a name used by Benjamin Franklin for his almanac.

It was not until the summer of 1779 that Jones was able to set sail. His ship had thirty-six guns, such as they were, and he had with him three other ships under French officers—the "Alliance," the "Pallas," and the "Vengeance." Among his crew were a hundred American sailors, who had just been set free from English prisons. And his master's mate, Richard Dale, a man of his own sort, had just escaped from prison in England.

Away they went, east and west, north and south, around the British isles, seeking for the men-of-war which should have swarmed in those seas, but finding only merchant vessels, a number of which were captured and their crews kept as prisoners. But the gallant commodore soon got tired of this. He had come out to fight, and he wanted to find something worth fighting. At length, on September 23d, he came in view of a large fleet of merchant ships, forty-two in all, under the charge of two frigates, the "Serapis," of forty-two guns, and the "Countess of Scarborough," of twenty-two smaller guns.

Commodore Jones left the smaller vessel for his consorts to deal with, and dashed away for the"Serapis" as fast as the tub-like "Bon Homme Richard" could go. The British ship was much stronger than his in number and weight of guns, but he cared very little for that. The "Serapis" had ten 18-

pound cannon in each battery, and the "Bon Homme Richard" only three. And these were such sorry excuses for cannon that two of them burst at the first fire, killing and wounding the most of their crews. After that Jones did all his fighting with 12 and 8-pound guns; that is, with guns which fired balls of these weights.

It was night when the battle began. Soon the 18-pounders of the "Serapis" were playing havoc with the sides of the "Bon Homme Richard." Many of the balls went clear through her and plunged into the sea beyond. Some struck her below the water level, and soon the rotten old craft was "leaking like a basket."

It began to look desperate for Jones and his ship. He could not half reply to the heavy fire of the English guns, and great chasms were made in the ship's side, where the 18-pound balls tore out the timbers between the port holes.

Captain Pearson of the "Serapis" looked at his staggering and leaking enemy, and thought it about time for the battle to end.

"Have you surrendered?" he shouted across the water to Commodore Jones.

"I have not yet begun to fight," was the famous answer of the brave Paul Jones.

Surrender, indeed! I doubt if that word was in Paul Jones' dictionary. He would rather have let his vessel sink. The ships now drifted together, and by Jones' order the jib-boom of the "Serapis" was lashed to his mizzen-mast. This brought the ships so close side by side that the English gunners could not open their ports, and had to fire through them and blow them off. And the gunners on both sides had to thrust the handles of their rammers through the enemy's port holes, in order to load their guns.

Affairs were now desperate. The "Bon Homme Richard" was on fire in several places. Water was pouring into her through a dozen rents. It seemed as if she must sink or burn. Almost any man except Paul Jones would have given up the fight. I know I should, and I fancy most of you would have done the same. But there was no give up in that man's soul.

One would think that nothing could have been worse, but worse still was to come. In this crisis the "Alliance," one of Jones' small fleet, came up and fired two broadsides into the wounded flagship, killing a number of her crew. Whether this was done on purpose or by mistake is not known. The French captain did not like Commodore Jones, and most men think he played the traitor.

And another bad thing took place. There were two or three hundred English prisoners on the "Bon Homme Richard," taken from her prizes. One of the American officers, thinking that all was over, set these men free, and they came swarming up. At the same time one of the crew tried to haul down the flag and he cried to the British for quarter. Paul Jones knocked him down by flinging a pistol at his head. He might sink or burn—but give up the ship? never!

The tide of chance now began to turn. Richard Dale, the master's mate, told the English prisoners that the vessel was sinking, and set them at work pumping and fighting the fire to save their lives. And one of the marines, who was fighting on the yard-arms, dropped a hand grenade into an open hatch of the "Serapis." It set fire to a heap of gun cartridges that lay below, and these exploded, killing twenty of the gunners and wounding many more, while the ship was set on fire. This ended the fight. The fire of the marines from the mast-tops had cleared the decks of the "Serapis" of men. Commodore Jones aided in this with the 9-pounders on his deck, loading and firing them himself. Captain Pearson stood alone, and when he heard the roar of the explosion he could bear the strain no longer. He ran and pulled down the flag, which had been nailed to the mast.

"Cease firing," said Paul Jones.

The "Serapis" was his. Well and nobly had it been won.

Never had there been a victory gained in such straits. The "Bon Homme Richard" was fast settling down into the sea. Pump as they would, they could never save her. Inch by inch she sank deeper. Jones and his gallant crew boarded the "Serapis," and at nine o'clock the next morning the noble old craft sank beneath the ocean waves, laden with honor, and with her victorious flag still flying. The "Serapis" was brought safely into port.

Captain Pearson had fought bravely, and the British ministry made him a knight for his courage.

"If I had a chance to fight him again I would make him a lord," said brave Paul Jones.

Never before or since has a victory been won under such desperate circumstances as those of Paul Jones, with his sinking and burning ship, his bursting guns, his escaped prisoners, and his treacherous consort. It was a victory to put his name forever on the annals of fame.

CHAPTER XIV

MARION THE SWAMP FOX AND GENERAL GREENE

FAR away back in old English history there was a famous archer named Robin Hood, who lived in the deep woods with a bold band of outlaws like himself. He and his band were foes of the nobles and friends of the poor, and his name will never be forgotten by the people of England.

No doubt you have read about the gallant archer. No man of his time could send an arrow so straight and sure as he. But we need not go back for hundreds of years to find our Robin Hood. We have had a man like him in our own country, who fought for us in the Revolution. His name was Francis Marion, and he was known as the "Swamp Fox"; for he lived in the swamps of South Carolina as Robin Hood did in the forests of England, and he was the stinging foe of the oppressors of the people.

I have already told you about the war in the North, and of how the British, after doing all they could to overthrow Washington and conquer the country, found themselves shut up in the cityof New York, with Washington like a watch-dog outside.

When the British generals found that the North was too hard a nut to crack, they thought they would try what they could do in the South. So they sent a fleet and an army down the coast, and before long they had taken the cities of Savannah and Charleston, and had their soldiers marching all over Georgia and South Carolina. General Gates, the man to whom Burgoyne surrendered, came down with a force of militia to fight them, but he was beaten so badly that he had to run away without a soldier to follow him. You can imagine that the British were proud of their success. They thought themselves masters of the South, and fancied they had only to march north and become masters there, too.

But you must not think that they were quite masters. Back in the woods and the swamps were men with arms in their hands and with love of country in their hearts. They were like wasps or hornets, who kept darting out from their nests, stinging the British troops, and then darting back out of sight. These gallant bands were led by Marion, Sumter, Pickens, and other brave men; but Marion's band was the most famous of them all, so I shall tell you about the Swamp Fox and what he did.

I fancy all of my young friends would havelaughed if they had seen Marion's band when it joined General Gates' army. Such scarecrows of soldiers they were! There were only about twenty of them in all, some of them white and some black, some men and some boys, dressed in rags that fluttered in the wind, and on horses that looked as if they had been fed on corncobs instead of corn.

Gates and his men did laugh at them, though they took care not to laugh when Marion was at hand. He was a small man, with a thin face, and dressed not much better than his men. But there was a look in his eye that told the soldiers he was not a safe man to laugh at.

Marion and his men were soon off again on a scout, and after Gates and his army had been beaten and scattered to the winds, they went back to their hiding places in the swamps to play the hornet once more.

Along the Pedee River these swamps extended for miles. There were islands of dry land far within, but they could only be reached by narrow paths which the British were not able to find. Only men who had spent their lives in that country could make their way safely through this broad stretch of water plants and water-soaked ground.

Marion's force kept changing. Now it went down to twenty men, now up to a hundred or more. It was never large, for there was not food or shelterfor many men. But there were enough of them to give the British plenty of trouble. They had their sentries on the outlook, and when a party of British or Tories went carelessly past out would spring Marion's men, send their foes flying like deer, and then back they would go before a strong body of the enemy could reach them.

These brave fellows had many hiding places in the swamps and many paths out of them. To-day they might strike the British in one place and to-morrow in another many miles away. Small as their force was they gave the enemy far more trouble than Gates had done with all his army. Marion's headquarters was a tract of land known as Snow's Island, where a creek ran into the Pedee. It was high and dry, was covered with trees and thickets, and was full of game. And all around it spread the soaking swamp, with paths known only to the patriot band. Among all their hiding places, this was their chosen home.

You may be sure that the British did their best to capture a man who gave them so much trouble as Marion. They sent Colonel Wemyss, one of their best cavalry officers, to hunt him down. Marion was then far from his hiding place and Wemyss got on his trail. But the Swamp Fox was hard to catch. He lead the British a lively chase, and when they gave it up in despair he followed them back. He came upon a large body ofTories and struck them so suddenly that hardly a man of them escaped, while he lost only one man. Tories, you should know, were Americans who fought on the British side.

The next man who tried to capture Marion was Colonel Tarleton, a hard rider and a good soldier, but a cruel and brutal man. He was hated in the South as much as Benedict Arnold was in the North. There is a good story told about how he was tricked by one of Marion's men. One day as he and his men were riding furiously along they came up to an old farmer, who was hoeing in his field beside the road.

"Can you tell me what became of the man who galloped by here just ahead of us?" asked one of them. "I will give you fifty pounds if you put me on his track."

"Do you mean the man on a black horse with a white star in its forehead?" asked the farmer.

"Yes, that's the fellow."

"He looked to me like Jack Davis, one of Marion's men, but he went past so fast that I could not be sure."

"Never mind who he was. What we want to know is where to find him."

"Bless your heart! he was going at such a pace that he couldn't well stop under four or five miles. I'm much afeard I can't earn that fifty pounds."

On rode the troop, and back into the woodswent the farmer. He had not gone far before he came to a black horse with a white star in its forehead. This he mounted and rode away. The farmer was Jack Davis himself.

That was the kind of men Tarleton had to deal with, and you may be sure that he did not catch any of them. He had his hunt, but he caught no game.

While Marion was keeping the war alive in South Carolina, an army was gathering under General Greene, who was, next to Washington, the best of the American generals. With him were Daniel Morgan, a famous leader of riflemen, William Washington, a cousin of the commander-in-chief, and Henry Lee, or "Light-horse Harry," father of the famous General Lee of the Civil War.

General Greene got together about two thousand men, half armed and half supplied and knowing nothing about war, so that he had a poor chance of defeating the trained British soldiers. But he was a Marion on a larger scale, and knew when to retreat and when to advance. I must tell you what he did.

In the first place Morgan the rifleman met the bold Colonel Tarleton and gave him a sound flogging. Tarleton hurried back to Lord Cornwallis, the British commander in the South. Cornwallis thought he would catch Morgan napping, but thelively rifleman was too wide-awake for him. He hurried back with the prisoners he had taken from Tarleton, and crossed the Catawba River just as the British came up. That night it rained hard, and the river rose so that it could not be crossed for three days.

General Greene now joined Morgan, and the retreat continued to the Yadkin River. This, too, was crossed by the Americans and a lucky rain again came up and swelled the river before the British could follow. When the British got across there was a race for the Dan River on the borders of Virginia. Greene got there first, crossed the stream, and held the fords or crossing-place against the foe. Cornwallis by this time had enough of it. Provisions were growing scarce, and he turned back. But he soon had Greene on his track, and he did not find his march a very comfortable one.

Here I must tell you an interesting anecdote about General Greene. Once, during his campaign, he entered a tavern at Salisbury, in North Carolina. He was wet to the skin from a heavy rain. Steele, the landlord, knew him and looked at him in surprise.

"Why, general, you are not alone?" he asked.

"Yes," said the general, "here I am, all alone, very tired, hungry, and penniless."

Mrs. Steele hastened to set a smoking hot mealbefore the hungry traveler. Then, while he was eating, she drew from under her apron two bags of silver and laid them on the table before him.

"Take these, general," she said. "You need them and I can do without them."

You may see that the women as well as the men of America did all they could for liberty, for there were many others like Mrs. Steele.

I have told you that General Greene was one of the ablest of the American leaders, and you have seen how he got the best of Cornwallis in the retreat. Several times afterwards he fought with the British. He was always defeated. His country soldiers could not face the British veterans. But each time he managed to get as much good from the fight as if he had won a victory, and by the end of the year the British were shut up in Charleston and Savannah, and the South was free again.

Where was Cornwallis during this time? Greene had led him so far north that he concluded to march on into Virginia and get the troops he would find there, and then come back. There was fighting going on in Virginia at this time. General Arnold, the traitor, was there, fighting against his own people. Against him was General Lafayette, a young French nobleman who had come to the help of the Americans.

I suppose some of you have read stories of how a wolf or some other wild animal walked into a trap, from which it could not get out again. Lord Cornwallis was not a wild animal, but he walked into just such a trap after he got to Virginia. When he reached there he took command of Arnold's troops. But he found himself not yet strong enough to face Lafayette, so he marched to Yorktown, near the mouth of York River, where he expected to get help by sea from New York. Yorktown was the trap he walked into, as you will see.

France had sent a fleet and an army to help the Americans, and just then this fleet came up from the West Indies and sailed into the Chesapeake, shutting off Yorktown from the sea. At the same time Washington, who had been closely watching what was going on, broke camp before New York and marched southward as fast as his men could go. Before Cornwallis could guess what was about to happen the trap was closed on him. In the bay near Yorktown was the strong French fleet; before Yorktown was the army of American and French soldiers.

There was no escape. The army and the fleet bombarded the town. A week of this was enough for Lord Cornwallis. He surrendered his army, seven thousand strong, on October 19, 1781, and the war was at an end. America was free.

CHAPTER XV

THE VOYAGE OF OUR SHIP OF STATE

HAVE any of my young readers ever been to Europe? Likely enough some of you may have been, for even young folks cross the ocean now-a-days. It has come to be an easy journey, with our great and swift steamers. But in past times it was a long and difficult journey, in which the ship was often tossed by terrible storms, and sometimes was broken to pieces on the rocks or went to the bottom with all on board.

What I wish to say is, that those who come from Europe to this country leave countries that are governed by kings, and come to a country that is governed by the people. In some of the countries of Europe the people might almost as well be slaves, for they have no vote and no one to speak for them, and the man who rules them is born to power. Even in England, which is the freest of them all, there is a king and queen and a House of Lords who are born to power. The people can vote, but only for members of the House of Commons. They have nothing to do with the monarch or the lords.

Of course you all know that this is not the case in our country. Here every man in power is put there by the votes of the people. As President Lincoln said, we have a government "of the people, by the people, and for the people."

We did not have such a government before the 4th of July, 1776. Our country was then governed by a king, and, what was worse, this king was on the other side of the ocean, and cared nothing for the people of America except as money bags to fill his purse. But after that 4th of July we governed ourselves, and had no king for lord and master; and we have got along very well without one.

Now you can see what the Declaration of Independence and the Revolution meant. With the Declaration we cut loose from England. Our ship of state set out on its long voyage to liberty. The Declaration cut the chain that fastened this great ship to England's shores. The Revolution was like the stormy passage across the ocean waves. At times it looked as if our ship of state would be torn to pieces by the storms, or driven back to the shores from which it set sail; but then the clouds would break and the sun shine, and onward our good ship would speed. At length it reached the port of liberty, and came to anchor far away from the land of kings.

This is a sort of parable. I think every oneof you will know what it means. The people of this country had enough of kings and their ways, and of being taxed without their consent. They made up their minds to be free to tax and govern themselves. It was for this they fought in the Revolution, and they won liberty with their blood.

And now, before we go on with the history of our country, it will be wise to stop and ask what kind of government the Americans gave themselves. They had thrown overboard the old government of kings. They had to make a new government of the people. I hope you do not think this was an easy task. If an architect or builder is shown a house and told to build another like that, he finds it very easy to do. But if he is shown a heap of stone and bricks and wood and told to build out of them a good strong house unlike any he has ever seen, he will find his task a very hard one, and may spoil the house in his building.

That was what our people had to do. They could have built a king's government easily enough. They had plenty of patterns to follow for that. But they had no pattern for a people's government, and, like the architect and his house, they might spoil it in the making. The fact is, this is just what they did. Their first government was spoiled in the making, and they had to take it down and build it over again.

This was done by what we call a Convention, made up of men called "delegates" sent by the several states. The Convention met in Philadelphia in 1787 for the purpose of forming a Constitution; that is, a plan of government under which the people should live and which the states and their citizens should have to obey.

This Convention was a wonderful body of statesmen. Its like has not often been seen. The wisest and ablest men of all the states were sent to it. They included all the great men—some we know already, Washington, Franklin, Jefferson, and Adams and many others of fine ability. For four months these men worked in secret. It was a severe task they had to perform, for some wanted one thing and some another, and many times it looked as if they would never agree; but at length all disputes were settled and their long labors were at an end.

General Washington was president of the Convention, and back of the chair on which he sat the figure of the sun was painted on the wall. When it was all over, Benjamin Franklin pointed to this painting and said to those who stood near him:

"Often while we sat here, troubled by hopes and fears, I have looked towards that figure, and asked myself if it was a rising or a setting sun. Now I know that it is the rising sun."

The rising sun indeed it was, for when the Conventionhad finished its work it had formed the noble Constitution under which we now live, the greatest state paper which man has ever formed.

But I fancy you want to know more about the noble framework of government built by the wise men of the Convention of 1787.

After the Union was formed there were thirteen states still, but each of these had lost some of its old powers. The powers taken from the states were given to the general government. Every state had still the right to manage its own affairs, but such things as concerned the whole people were managed by the general government.

What were these things? Let us see. There was the power to coin money, to lay taxes, to control the post-office, and to make laws for the good of the whole nation. And there was the power to form an army and navy, to make treaties with other countries, and to declare war if we could not get on in peace.

Under the Confederation which was formed during the Revolutionary War, the states could do these things for themselves; under the Constitution they could do none of these things, but they could pass laws that affected only themselves, and could tax their own people for state purposes.

I have spoken several times of the general government. No doubt you wish to know what this government was like. Well, it was made up ofthree bodies, one of which made laws for the people, the second considered if these laws agreed with the Constitution, the third carried out these laws, or put them in force.

The body that made the laws was named the Congress of the United States. It consisted of two sections. One was called the Senate, and was made up of two members from each state. As we have now more than forty-five states the Senate at present has more than ninety members. The other section was called the House of Representatives, and its members were voted for directly by the people. The members of the Senate were voted for by the legislatures of the states, who had been elected by the people.

All the laws were to be made by Congress, but not one of them could become a law until it was approved by the President. If he did not approve of a law, he vetoed it, that is, he returned it without being signed with his name, and then it could not be enforced as a law until voted for by two-thirds of the members of Congress.

It was the duty of the President to execute or carry out the laws. He took the place of the king in other countries. But he was not born to his position like a king, but had to be voted for by the people, and could stay in office for four years only. Then he, or some one else, had to be voted for again.

Next to the President was the Vice-President, who was to take his place if he should die or resign. While the President was in office the Vice-President had nothing to do except to act as presiding officer of the Senate. What we call the Cabinet are persons chosen by the President to help him in his work. You must understand that it takes a number of leading men and a great many men under these to do all the work needed to carry on our government.

The third body of our government was called the Supreme Court. This was made up of some of the ablest lawyers and judges of the country. They were not to be voted for, but to be chosen by the President and then approved by the Senate. The duty of the Supreme Court is to consider any law brought to its notice and decide if it agrees with the Constitution. If the Court decides that a law is not constitutional, it ceases to be of any effect.

This is not so very hard to understand, is it? The President and Congress elected by the people; the Supreme Court and Cabinet selected by the President; the Constitution the foundation of our government; and the laws passed by Congress the building erected on the foundation.

Its great feature is that it is a republic—a government "of the people, by the people, and for the people." Ours is not the first republic. Therehave been others. But it is the greatest. It is the only one that covers half a continent, and is made up of states many of which are larger than some of the kingdoms of Europe. For more than a hundred years the Constitution made in 1787 has held good. Then it covered thirteen states and less than four million people; now it covers more than forty-five states and eighty million people. Then it was very poor, and had a hard struggle before it; now it is very rich and prosperous. It has grown to be the richest country in the world and one of the greatest.

CHAPTER XVI

THE END OF A NOBLE LIFE

EVERY four years a great question arises in this country, and all the states and their people are disturbed until this question is settled. Even business nearly stops still, for many persons can think of nothing but the answer to this question.

Who shall be President? That is the question which at the end of every four years troubles the minds of our people. This question was asked for the first time in 1789, after the Constitution had been made and accepted by the states, but this time the people found it a very easy question to answer.

There were several men who had taken a great part in the making of our country, and who might have been named for President. One of these was Thomas Jefferson, who wrote the Declaration of Independence. Another of them was Benjamin Franklin, who got France to come to our aid, and did many other noble things for his country. But none of them stood so high in the respect and admiration of the people as George Washington,who had led our armies through the great war, and to whom, more than to any other man, we owed our liberty.

This time, then, there was no real question as to whom should be President. Washington was the man. All men, all parties, settled upon Washington. No one opposed him; there was no man in the country like him. He was unanimously elected the first President of the United States.

In olden times, when a victorious general came back to Rome with the splendid spoils brought from distant countries, the people gave him a triumph, and all Rome rose to do him honor and to gaze upon the splendor of the show. Washington had no splendid spoils to display. But he had the love of the people, which was far better than gold and silver won in war; and all the way from his home at Mount Vernon to New York, where he was to take the office of President, the people honored him with a triumph.

Along the whole journey, men, women and children crowded the roadside, and waited for hours to see him pass. That was before the day of railroads, and he had to go slowly in his carriage, so that everybody had a fine chance to see and greet him as he went by. Guns were fired as he passed through the towns; arches of triumph were erected for his carriage to go under; flowers were strewn in the streets for its wheels to roll over;cheers and cries of greeting filled the air; all that the people could do to honor their great hero was done.

On the 30th of April, 1789, Washington took the oath of office as the first President of our country and people. He stood on the balcony of a building in front of Federal Hall, in which Congress met, and in the street before him was a vast multitude, full of joy and hope. When he had taken the oath cannon roared out, bells were rung in all the neighboring steeples, and a mighty shout burst from the assembled multitude:

"Long live George Washington, President of the United States!"

This, I have said, was in New York. But Philadelphia was soon chosen as the seat of government, and the President and Congress moved to that city the next year. There they stayed for ten years. In the year 1800 a new city, named Washington, on the banks of the Potomac, was made the capital of our country, and in that city Congress has met ever since.

I must say something here about another of the great men of Revolutionary times, Alexander Hamilton. He was great in financial or money matters, and this was very important at that time, for the money-affairs of the country were in a sad state.

In the Revolution our people had very littlemoney, and that was one reason why they had so much suffering. Congress soon ran out of gold and silver, so it issued paper money. This did very well for a time, and in the end a great deal of paper money was set afloat, but people soon began to get afraid of it. There was too much money of this kind for so poor a country. The value of the Continental currency, as it was called, began to go down, and the price of everything else to go up. In time the paper money lost almost all its value.

Such was the money the people had at the end of the Revolution. It was not good for much, was it? But it was the only kind of money Congress had to pay the soldiers with or to pay the other debts of the government. The country owed much more money than it could pay, so that it was what we call bankrupt. Nobody would trust it or take its paper in payment. What Alexander Hamilton did was to help the country to pay its debts and to bring back its lost credit, and in doing that he won great honor.

Hamilton came to this country from the West Indies during the Revolution. He was then only a boy, but he soon showed himself a good soldier, and Washington made him an officer on his staff and one of his friends. He often asked young Hamilton for advice, and took it, too.

Hamilton was one of the men who made theConstitution, and when Washington became President he chose him as his Secretary of the

Treasury. That is, he gave him the money affairs of the government to look after. Hamilton was not afraid of the load of debt, and he soon took off its weight. He asked Congress to pay not only its own debt, but that of the states as well, and also to make good all the paper money. Congress did not like to do this, but Hamilton talked to the members till he persuaded them to do so.

Then he set himself to pay it. He laid a tax on whiskey and brandy and on all goods that came into the country. He had a mint, which is a building where money is coined from metal, and a national bank built in Philadelphia. He made the debt a government fund or loan, on which he agreed to pay interest, and to pay off the principal as fast as possible. It was not long before all the fund was taken up by those who had money, and the country got back its lost credit, for the taxes began to bring in much money.

Washington was President for eight years. That made two terms of four years each. Many wished to make him President for a third term, but he refused to run again. Since then no one has been made President for more than two terms.

George Washington had done enough for his country. He loved his home, but he had little time to live there. When he was only a boy hewas called away to take part in the French and Indian War. Then, after spending some happy years at home, he was called away again to lead the army in the Revolutionary War. Finally, he served his country eight years as President.

He was now growing old and wanted rest, and he went back with joy to his beloved home at Mount Vernon, hoping to spend there the remainder of his days. But trouble arose with France, and it looked as if there would be a new war, and Washington was asked to take command of the army again. He consented, though he had had enough of fighting; but fortunately the war did not come, so he was not obliged to abandon his home.

He died in December, 1799, near the end of the century of which he was one of the greatest men. The news of his death filled all American hearts with grief. Not while the United States exists will the name of Washington be forgotten or left without honor. His home and tomb at Mt. Vernon are visited each year by thousands of patriotic Americans. As was said of him long ago by General Henry Lee, he was and is, "first in war, first in peace, and first in the hearts of his countrymen."

CHAPTER XVII

THE STEAMBOAT AND THE COTTON GIN

I THINK you must now have learned a great deal about the history of your country from the time Columbus crossed the ocean till the year 1800, the beginning of the Nineteenth century. You have been told about discovery, and settlement, and wars, and modes of life, and government, and other things, but you must bear in mind that these are not the whole of history. The story of our country is broad and deep enough to hold many other things beside these. For instance, there is the story of our great inventors, to whom we owe so much. I propose in this chapter to tell you about some of those who lived near the year 1800.

First, I must ask you to go back with me to a kitchen in Scotland many years ago. On the open hearth of that kitchen a bright fire blazed, and near by sat a thoughtful-faced boy, with his eyes fixed on the tea-kettle which was boiling away over the fire, while its lid kept lifting to let the steam escape. His mother, who was bustling about, no doubt thought him idle, and may havescolded him a little. But he was far from idle; he was busy at work—not with his hands, but with his brain. The brain, you know, may be hard at work while the body is doing nothing.

How many of you have seen the lid of a kettle of boiling water keeping up its clatter as the steam lifts it and puffs out into the air? And what thought has this brought into your mind? Into the mind of little James Watt, the Scotch boy, it brought one great thought, that of power. As he looked at it, he said to himself that the steam which comes from boiling water must have a great deal of force, if a little of it could keep the kettle lid clattering up and down; and he asked himself if such a power could not be put to some good use.

Our Scotch boy was not the first one to have that thought. Others had thought the same thing, and steam had been used to move a poor sort of engine. But what James Watt did when he grew up, was to invent a much better engine than had ever been made before. It was a great day for us all when that engine was invented. Before that time men had done most of the work of the world with their hands, and you may imagine that the work went on very slowly. Since that time most of the world's work has been done with the aid of the steam-engine, and one man can do as much as many men could do in the past. You have seen the wheels rolling and heard the machinesrattling and the hammers clanging in our great factories and workshops. And I fancy most of you know that back of all these is the fire under the boilers and the steam in the engine, the mighty magician which sets all these wheels and machines at work and changes raw material into so many things of use and beauty.

Now let us come back to our American inventors. I have spoken about the steam engine because it was with this that most of them worked. They thought that if horses could drag a wagon over the ground and the wind could drive a vessel through the water, steam might do the same thing, and they set themselves to see in what way a carriage or a boat could be moved by a steam engine.

Very likely you have all heard about Robert Fulton and his steamboat, but you may not know that steamboats were running on American waters years before that of Fulton was built. Why, as long ago as 1768, before the Revolutionary War, Oliver Evans, one of our first inventors, had made a little boat which was moved by steam and paddle-wheels. Years afterwards he made a large engine for a boat at New Orleans. It was put in the boat, but there came a dry season and low water, so that the boat could not be used, and the owners took the engine out and set it to work on a sawmill. It did so well there that it was neverput back in the boat; so that steamboat never had a chance.

Oliver Evans was the first man to make a steamboat, but there were others who thought they could move a boat by steam. Some of these were in Europe and some in America. Down in Virginia was an inventor named Rumsey who moved a boat at the speed of four miles an hour. In this boat jets of water were pumped through the stern and forced the boat along. In Philadelphia was another man named John Fitch, who was the first man to make a successful steamboat. His boat was moved with paddles like an Indian canoe. It was put on the Delaware River, between Philadelphia and Trenton in 1790, and ran for several months as a passenger boat, at the speed of seven or eight miles an hour. Poor John Fitch! He was unfortunate and in the end he killed himself.

I am glad to be able to tell you a different story of the next man who tried to make a steamboat. His name was Robert Fulton. He was born in Pennsylvania, and as a boy was very fond of the water, he and the other boys having an old flatboat which they pushed along with a pole. Fulton got tired of this way of getting along, and like a natural-born inventor set his wits to work. In the end he made two paddle-wheels which hung over the sides and could be moved in the water byturning a crank and so force the boat onward. The boys found this much easier than the pole, and likely enough young Fulton thought a large vessel might be moved in the same way.

He knew all about what others had done. He had heard how Rumsey moved his boat by pumping water through the stern, and Fitch by paddling it along. And he had seen a boat in Scotland moved by a stern paddle-wheel. I fancy he had not forgotten the side paddle-wheel he made as a boy to go fishing with, for when he set out to invent his steamboat this is the plan he tried.

Fulton made his first boat in France, but he had bad luck there. Then he came to America and built a boat in New York. While he was at work on this boat in America, James Watt, of whom I have already told you, was building him an engine in England. He wanted the best engine that he could get, and he thought the Scotch inventor was the right man to make it.

While Fulton was working some of the smart New Yorkers were laughing. They called his boat "Fulton's Folly," and said it would not move faster than the tide would carry it. But he let them laugh and worked on, and at last, one day in 1807, the new boat, which he named the "Clermont," was afloat in the Hudson ready for trial. Hundreds of curious people came to see it start. Some were ready to laugh again when they saw theboat, with its clumsy paddle-wheels hanging down in the water on both sides. They were not covered with wooden frames as were such wheels afterwards.

"That boat move? So will a log move if set adrift," said the people who thought themselves very wise. "It will move when the tide moves it, and not before." But none of them felt like laughing when they saw the wheels begin to turn and the boat to glide out into the stream, moving against the tide.

"She moves! she moves!" cried the crowd, and nobody said a word about "Fulton's Folly."

Move she did. Up the Hudson she went against wind and current, and reached Albany, one hundred and forty-two miles away, in thirty-two hours. This was at the rate of four and a half miles an hour. It was not many years before steamboats were running on all our rivers.

That is all I shall say here about the steamboat, for there is another story of invention I wish to tell you before I close. This is about the cotton fibre, which you know is the great product of the Southern States.

The cotton plant when ripe has a white, fluffy head, and a great bunch of snow-white fibres, within which are the seeds. In old times these had to be taken out by hand, and it was a whole day's work for a negro to get the seeds out of apound of the cotton. This made cotton so dear that not much of it could be sold. In 1784 eight bags of it were sent to Liverpool, and the custom-house people there seized it for duties. They said it must have been smuggled from some other country, for the United States could not have produced such a "prodigious quantity."

A few years afterwards a young man named Eli Whitney went South to teach in a private family, but before he got there some one else had his situation, and he was left with nothing to do. Mrs. Greene, the widow of General Greene, who fought so well in the Revolution, took pity on him and gave him a home in her house. He paid her by fixing up things about her house. She found him so handy that she asked him if he could not invent a machine to take the seeds out of the cotton. Whitney said he would try, and he set himself to work. It was not long before he had a machine made which did the work wonderfully well. This machine is known as the "cotton-gin," or cotton engine, for gin is short for engine. On one side of it are wires so close together that the seeds cannot get through. Between them are circular saws which catch the cotton and draw it through, while the seeds pass on.

The machine was a simple one, but it acted like magic. A hundred negroes could not clean as much cotton in a day as one machine. The price of cotton soon went down and a demand for it sprang up. In 1795, when the cotton gin was made, only about 500,000 pounds of cotton were produced in this country. By 1801 this had grown to 20,000,000 pounds. Now it has grown to more than 12,000,000 bales, of nearly 500 pounds each. This is sold to foreign countries and is worked in our own mills at home, being made into millions of yards of cloth of many kinds to clothe the people of the earth. All this comes from the work of Eli Whitney's machine. And the seed taken from the cotton is pressed for the oil it contains, so that from a year's crop we get nearly 150,000,000 gallons of useful oil.

CHAPTER XVIII

THE ENGLISH AND AMERICANS FIGHT AGAIN

FOR years before and after the year 1800 all Europe was filled with war and bloodshed. Most of my readers must have heard of Napoleon Bonaparte, one of the greatest generals that ever lived, and one of the most cruel men. He was at the head of the armies of France, and was fighting all Europe. England was his greatest enemy and fought him on land and sea, and this fighting on the sea made trouble between England and the United States.

The English wanted men for their war-vessels and said they had a right to take Englishmen wherever they could find them. So they began to take sailors off of American merchant vessels. They said that these men were deserters from the British navy, but the fact is that many of them were true-born Americans; and our people grew very angry as this went on year after year.

What made it worse was the insolence of some of the British captains. One of them went so far as to stop an American war-vessel, the "Chesapeake,"and demand part of her crew, who, he said, were British deserters. When Captain Barron refused to give them up the British captain fired all his guns and killed and wounded numbers of the American crew. The "Chesapeake" had no guns fit to fire back, so her flag had to be pulled down and the men to be given up.

You may well imagine that this insult made the American blood boil. There would have been war at that time if the British government had not owned that it was wrong and offered to pay for the injury. A few years afterwards the insult was paid for in a different way. Another proud British captain thought he could treat Americans in the same saucy fashion. The frigate "President" met the British sloop-of-war "Little Belt," and hailed it, the captain calling through his trumpet, "What ship is that?"

Instead of giving a civil reply the British captain answered with a cannon shot. Then the "President" fired a broadside which killed eleven and wounded twenty-one men on the "Little Belt." When the captain of the "President" hailed again the insolent Briton was glad to reply in a more civil fashion. He had been taught a useful lesson.

The United States was then a poor country, and not in condition to go to war. But no nation could submit to such insults as these. It is saidthat more than six thousand sailors had been taken from our merchant ships, and among these were two nephews of General Washington, who were seized while they were on their way home from Europe, and put to work as common seamen on a British war-vessel.

At length, on June 18, 1812, the United States declared war against Great Britain. It had put up with insults and injuries as long as it could bear them. It did not take long to teach the haughty British captains that American sea-dogs were not to be played with. The little American fleet put to sea, and before the end of the year it had captured no less than five of the best ships in the British navy and had not lost a single ship in return. I fancy the people of England quit singing their proud song, "Britannia rules the waves."

Shall I tell you the whole story of this war? I do not think it worth while, for there is much of it you would not care to hear. The war went on for two years and a half, on sea and land, but there were not many important battles, and the United States did not win much honor on land. But on the sea the sailors of our country covered themselves with glory.

Most of the land battles were along the borders of Canada. Here there was a good deal of fighting, but most of it was of no great account. At first the British had the best of it, and then theAmericans began to win battles, but it all came to an end about where it began. Neither side gained anything for the men that were killed.

There was one naval battle in the north that I must tell you about. On Lake Erie the British had a fleet of six war-vessels, and for a time they had everything their own way. Then Captain Oliver Perry, a young officer, was sent to the lake to build a fleet and fight the British.

When he got there the stuff for his ships was growing in the woods. He had to cut down trees and build ships from their timber. But he worked like a young giant, and very soon had some vessels built and afloat. He found some also on the lake, and in a wonderfully short time he had a fleet on the lake and was sailing out to find the British war-ships.

The fleets met on September 10, 1813. The Americans had the most vessels, but the British had the most guns, and soon they were fighting like sea-dragons. The "Lawrence," Captain Perry's flagship, fought two of the largest British ships till it was nearly ready to sink, and so many of its crew were killed and wounded that it had only eight men left fit for fighting. What do you think the brave Perry did then? He leaped into a small boat and was rowed away, with the American flag floating in his hand, though the British ships were firing hotly at him.

When he reached the "Niagara," another of his ships, he sprang on board and sailed right through the enemy's fleet, firing right and left into their shattered vessels. The British soon had enough of this, and in fifteen minutes more they gave up the fight.

"We have met the enemy and they are ours," wrote Perry to General Harrison. He was a born hero of the waves.

Now I think we had better take a look out to sea and learn what was going on there. We did not have many ships, but they were like so many bulldogs in a flock of sheep. The whole world looked on with surprise to see our little fleet of war-vessels making such havoc in the proud British navy which no country in Europe had ever been able to defeat.

In less than two months after war was declared the frigate "Essex" met the British sloop-of-war "Alert" and took it in eight minutes, without losing a man. The "Essex" was too strong for the "Alert," but six days afterwards the "Constitution" met the "Guerriere," and these vessels were nearly the same in size. But in half an hour the "Guerriere" was nearly shot to pieces and ready to sink, and had lost a hundred of her men. The others were hastily taken off, and then down went the proud British frigate to the bottom of the Gulf of St. Lawrence.

All the island of Great Britain went into mourning when it learned how the Americans had served this good ship. There was soon more to mourn for. The American sloop "Wasp" captured the British sloop "Frolic." The frigate "United States" captured the frigate "Macedonian." The "Constitution" met the "Java" and served it the same way as it had done the "Guerriere." In two hours the "Java" was a wreck. Soon after the sloop "Hornet" met the ship "Peacock" and handled her so severely that she sank while her crew was being taken off.

Later on the British won two battles at sea, and that was all they gained during the whole war. On the water the honors stayed with the Americans.

There was one affair in which the British won great dishonor instead of honor. In July, 1814, a strong British fleet sailed up Chesapeake Bay, with an army of nearly five thousand men on board. These were landed and marched on the city of Washington, the capital of the young republic.

Their coming was a surprise. There were few trained soldiers to meet this army, and those were not the days of railroads, so that no troops could be brought in haste from afar. Those that gathered were nearly all raw militia, and they did not stand long before the British veterans who had fought in the wars with Napoleon. They weresoon put to flight, and the British army marched into our capital city.

There they behaved in a way that their country has ever since been ashamed of. They set fire to the public buildings and burned most of them to the ground. The Capitol, the President's house, and other buildings were burned, and the records of the government were destroyed. Then, having acted like so many savages, the British hurried away before the Americans could get at them for revenge. That was a victory, I fancy, which the British do not like to read about.

They had been so successful at Washington that they thought they would try the same thing with another city. This time they picked out New Orleans, which was so far away from the thickly settled part of the country that they fancied it would be an easy matter to capture it. In this they made a great mistake, as you will soon see.

There was a general in the South who was not used to being defeated. This was Andrew Jackson, one of our bravest soldiers, who had just won fame in a war with the Indians of Georgia. He was a man who was always ready to fight and this the English found when they marched on New Orleans. There were twelve thousand of them, and Jackson, who had been sent there to meet them, only had half that many. And the British were trained soldiers, while the Americanswere militia. But most of them were men of the backwoods, who knew how to shoot.

THE BATTLE OF NEW ORLEANS.

Some of you may have heard that Jackson's men fought behind cotton bales. That is not quite true, but he was in such a hurry in building his breastworks that he did put in them some bales of cotton taken from the warehouses. The British, who were in as great a hurry, built a breastwork of sugar hogsheads which they found on the plantations. But the cannon balls soon set the cotton on fire and filled the air with flying sugar, so the bales and the hogsheads had to be pulled out. It was found that cotton and sugar, while good enough in their place, were not good things to stop cannon balls.

Soon the British marched against the American works, and there was a terrible fight.

"Stand to your guns, my men," said Jackson to his soldiers. "Make every shot tell. Give it to them."

Many of the men were old hunters from Tennessee, some of whom could hit a squirrel in the eye, and when they fired the British fell in rows. Not a man could cross that terrible wall of fire, and they fought on until twenty-six hundred of them lay bleeding on the field, while only eight Americans were killed.

That ended the battle. The men were not born who could face a fire like that. It ended the waralso, and it was the last time Americans and Englishmen ever fought each other. Jackson became the hero of the country, and he was finally elected President of the United States. I cannot say that he was well fitted to be President. He was a very obstinate man, who always wanted to have his own way, and that is better in a soldier than in a President. But he was one who loved his country, and when one of the states of the South sought to secede from the Union, Jackson, though he was a son of the South himself, quickly gave the seceders to understand that he was a general as well as a President, and that no state should leave the ranks of the Union while he marched at its head.

CHAPTER XIX

HOW THE VICTIMS OF THE ALAMO WERE REVENGED

I HAVE told you the story of more than one war. I shall have to tell you now about still another in which the Americans fought the Mexicans in Texas.

I suppose you know that Texas is one of our states, and the largest of them all. That is, it is largest in square miles; not in number of people. In former times it was part of Mexico, and was a portion of what is called Spanish America. But there came to be more Americans in it than Spaniards. People kept going there from the United States until it was much more of an American than a Spanish country.

General Santa Anna, who was at the head of the Mexican government at the time I speak of, was somewhat of a tyrant, and he tried to rule the people of Texas in a way they would not submit to. Then he ordered them to give up all their guns to his soldiers, but instead of that they took their guns and drove the Mexican soldiers away. After that there was war, as you might well suppose, for a Mexican army was sent to punish the Texans.

I wish now to tell you about what happened to some very brave Americans. There were only one hundred and seventy-five of them, and they were attacked by General Santa Anna with an army of several thousand men. But they were commanded by Colonel Travis, a brave young Texan, and among them was the famous David Crockett, a great hunter, and Colonel James Bowie, who invented the terrible "bowie-knife," and other bold and daring men who had settled in Texas. They had made a fort of an old Spanish building called the Alamo.

The kind of men I have named do not easily give up. The Mexicans poured bomb-shells and cannon balls into their fort, battering down the walls and killing many of them, but they fought on like tigers, determined to die rather than surrender. At length so many of them were dead that there were not enough left to defend the walls, and the Mexican soldiers captured the Alamo. The valiant Crockett kept on fighting, and when he fell, the ground before him was covered with Mexican dead. Then Santa Anna ordered his soldiers to shoot down all that were left. That is what is called the "Massacre of the Alamo."

It was not long before the Americans had their revenge. Their principal leader was a bold and able man named Samuel Houston. He had less than eight hundred men under him, but hemarched on the Mexicans, who had then about eighteen hundred men.

"Men, there is the enemy," said brave General Houston. "Do you wish to fight?"

"We do," they all shouted.

"Charge on them, then, for liberty or death! Remember the Alamo!"

"Remember the Alamo!" they cried, as they rushed onward with the courage of lions.

In a little time the Mexicans were running like frightened deer, and the daring Texans were like deer hounds on their tracks. Of the eighteen hundred Mexicans all but four hundred were killed, wounded, or taken prisoners, while the Americans lost only thirty men. They had well avenged the gallant Travis and the martyrs of the Alamo.

The cruel Santa Anna was taken prisoner. He had only one sound leg, and the story was that he was caught with his wooden leg stuck fast in the mud. Many of the Texans wanted to hang him for his murders at the Alamo, but in the end he was set free.

All this took place in 1835. Texas was made an independent country, the "Lone Star Republic," with General Houston for President. But its people did not want to stand alone. They were American born and wished to belong to the United States. So this country was asked to accept Texasas a state of the Union. Nine years after it was accepted as one of the American states.

Perhaps some of my readers may think that this story has much more to do with the history of Mexico than that of the United States. But the taking of Texas as a state was United States history, and so was what followed. You know how one thing leads to another. Mexico did not feel like giving up Texas so easily, and her rulers said that the United States had no right to take it. It was not long before the soldiers of the two countries met on the border lands and blood was shed. There was a sharp fight at a place called Palo Alto, and a sharper one at a place called Resaca de la Palma. In both of them the Mexicans were defeated.

Congress then declared war against Mexico, and very soon there was hard fighting going on elsewhere. General Zachary Taylor, a brave officer, who had fought the Seminole Indians in Florida, led the American troops across the Rio Grande River into Mexico, and some time afterwards marched to a place called Buena Vista. He had only five thousand men, while Santa Anna was marching against him with twenty thousand—four to one. General Taylor's army was in great danger. Santa Anna sent him a message, asking him to surrender if he did not want his army cut to pieces; but Rough and Ready, as Taylor's men called him, sent word back that he was there to fight, not to surrender.

The battle that followed was a desperate one. It took place on February 23, 1847. The Mexican lancers rode bravely against the American lines and were driven back at the cannon's mouth. For ten long hours the fighting went on. The Mexicans gained the high ground above the pass and put the American troops in danger. Charge after charge was made, but like bulldogs the Yankee soldiers held their ground. On came the dashing Mexican lancers, shouting their war-cry of "God and Liberty," and charging a battery commanded by Captain Bragg. The lancers captured some of the guns and drove the soldiers back. Captain Bragg sent a messenger in haste to General Taylor, saying that he must have more men or he could not hold his ground.

"I have no more men to send you," said Rough and Ready. "Give them a little more grape, Captain Bragg."

The cannon were loaded with grape-shot and fired into the ranks of the enemy, cutting great gaps through them. Again and again they were loaded and fired, and then the fine Mexican cavalry turned and fled. They could not stand any more of Captain Bragg's grape.

That night both armies went to sleep on the field of battle. But when the next day dawned the Mexicans were gone. Santa Anna had led them away during the night and General Taylor had won the greatest victory of the war. He received a noble reward for it, for the following year he was elected President of the United States.

The next thing done in this war was an attempt to capture the city of Mexico, the capital of the country. The easiest way to get there was by sea, for it was a long journey by land, so a fleet was got ready and an army sent south on the Gulf of Mexico. This army was led by General Winfield Scott, who had fought against the British in the War of 1812.

Onward they sailed till they came before the seaport city of Vera Cruz. This had a strong fort, which was battered for four days by the American cannon, when its walls were so shattered that the Mexicans gave it up. In this way a good starting-point was gained.

But I would have you all know that the Americans had no easy road before them. The city of Mexico lies in the center of the country on land that is as high as many mountains, and the way to it from the coast goes steadily upward, and has many difficult passes and rough places, where a small force might stop an army.

THE STORMING OF CHAPULTEPEC.

If the Mexicans had known their business and had possessed good generals I am afraid the Americans might never have gotten up this ruggedroad. The Mexicans had men enough but they wanted able leaders. At one of the passes, named Cerro Gordo, Santa Anna waited with 15,000 men. The Americans had only 9,000. It looked as if they might have to turn back.

What did they do? Why, they managed to drag a battery to the top of a steep hill that overlooked the pass. And while these guns poured their shot down on the astonished Mexicans the army attacked them in front. In a few hours they were in full flight. Five generals, and 3,000 men were taken prisoners, and Santa Anna himself came so near being taken that he left his cork leg behind. Do you not think a general ought to have two good legs when he has to run as often as Santa Anna had?

Onward they marched until not very far away lay the beautiful city of Mexico. But here and there along the road were strong forts, and Santa Anna had collected a large army, three times as large as that of the Americans. You may see that General Scott had a very hard task before him. But there is one way to get past forts without fighting; which is, to go around them. This is what General Scott did. He marched to the south, and soon he was within ten miles of the capital without a battle.

August 20th was a great day for the American army. That day our brave troops fought likeheroes, and before night they had won five victories. One of these was on a steep hill called Churubusco, which they charged up in the face of the Mexican guns. Then on they went, and in a short time the old city, the most ancient in America, was in their hands. That ended the war. When peace was made the United States claimed the provinces of New Mexico and California, which had been captured by our soldiers, but for which Mexico was paid a large sum. No one then dreamed how rich the provinces were in silver and gold. Not long after the gold of California was discovered, and that country, which had been feebly held by a few Mexicans, was quickly filled by an army of gold-seekers. Since then it has proved one of the richest parts of the earth.

CHAPTER XX

HOW SLAVERY LED TO WAR

ALL of my young readers must know what a wonderful age this is that we live in, and what marvelous things have been done. Some of you, no doubt, have read the stories of magic in the "Arabian Nights Entertainments," and thought them very odd, if not absurd. But if any one, a hundred years ago, had been told about the railroad, the telegraph, the photograph, the phonograph, vessels that run beneath the surface of the water, and ships that sail in the air, I fancy they would have called all this nonsense and "Arabian Nights" magic. Why, think of it, a trolley car is as magical, in its way, as Aladdin's wonderful lamp.

But while you know much about these things, there has been one great step of progress which, I fancy, you know or think very little about. I do not mean material but moral progress, for you must bear in mind that while the world has been growing richer it has also been growing better.

A hundred years ago many millions of men were held as slaves in America and Europe.Some of these were black and some were white, but they could be bought and sold like so many cattle, could be whipped by their masters, and had no more rights than so many brute beasts.

To-day there is not a slave in Europe or America. All these millions of slaves have been set free. Do you not think I am right in saying that the world has grown better as well as richer? Why, fifty years ago there were millions of slaves in our own country, and now there is not one in all the land. Is not that a great gain to mankind? But it is sad to think that this slavery gave rise to a terrible war. I shall have to tell you about this war, after I have told you how slavery brought it on.

In the early part of this book you read of how white men first came to this country. I have now to tell you that black men were brought here almost as soon. In 1619, just twelve years after Captain John Smith and the English colonists landed at Jamestown, a Dutch ship sailed up the James River and sold them some negroes to be held as slaves.

You remember about Pocahontas, the Indian girl who saved the life of Captain John Smith. She was afterwards married to John Rolfe, the man who first planted tobacco in Virginia. John Rolfe wrote down what was going on in Virginia, and it was he who told us about these negroesbrought in as slaves. This is what he wrote:

"About the last of August came in, a Dutch marine-of-war, that sold us 20 Negars."

These twenty "Negars," as he called them, grew in numbers until there were four million negro slaves in our country in 1860, when the war began. There are twice that many black people in the country to-day, but I am glad to be able to say that none of them are slaves. Yet how sad it is to think that it cost the lives of hundreds of thousands of men, and misery to multitudes of families, to set them free.

"Where did all these black men come from?" I am sure I hear some young voice asking that question. Well, they came from Africa, the land of the negroes. In our time merchant ships are used to carry goods from one country to another. In old times many of these ships were used in carrying negroes to be sold as slaves. The wicked captains would steal the poor black men in Africa, or buy them from the chiefs, who had taken them prisoners in war. Some of them filled their ships so full of these miserable victims that hundreds of them died and were thrown overboard. Then, when they got to the West Indies or to the shores of our country, they would sell all that were left alive to the planters, to spend the rest of their lives like oxen chained to the yoke.

It was a very sad and cruel business, but peoplethen thought it right, and some of the best men took part in it. That is why I say the world has grown better. We have a higher idea of right and wrong in regard to such things than our forefathers had.

Slaves were kept in all parts of the country, in the North as well as the South. There were more of them in the South than in the North, for they were of more use there as workers in the tobacco and rice and cotton fields. Most of those in the North were kept as house servants. Not many of them were needed in the fields.

The North had not much use for slaves, and in time laws were passed, doing away with slavery in all the Northern states. Very likely the same thing would have taken place in the South if it had not been for the discovery of the cotton-gin. I have told you what a change this great invention made. Before that time it did not pay to raise cotton in our fields. After that time cotton grew to be a very profitable crop, and the cultivation of it spread wider and wider until it was planted over a great part of the South.

This made a remarkable change. Negroes were very useful in the cotton fields, and no one in the South now thought of doing away with slavery. After 1808 no ships could bring slaves to this country, but there were a great many here then, and many others were afterwards born andgrew up as slaves, so that the numbers kept increasing year after year.

There were always some people, both in the North and the South, who did not like slavery. Among them were Franklin and Washington and Jefferson and other great men. In time there got to be so many of these people in the North that they formed what were called Anti-slavery Societies. Some of them said that slavery should be kept where it was and not taken into any new states. Others said that every slave in the United States ought to be set free.

This brought on great excitement all over the country. The people in the North who believed in slavery were often violent. Now and then there were riots. Buildings where Anti-slavery meetings were held were burned down. One of the leaders of the Abolitionists, as the Anti-slavery people were called, was dragged through the streets of Boston with a rope tied round his body, and would have been hanged if his friends had not got him away.

But as time went on the Abolitionists grew stronger in the North. Many slaves ran away from their masters, and these were hidden by their white friends until they could get to Canada, where they were safe. All through the South and North people were excited.

I do not think many of our people expected thecruel war that was coming. If they had they might have been more careful what they said and did. But for all that, war was close at hand, and two things helped to bring it on.

There had been fighting in Kansas, one of the territories that was to be made into a state, and among the fighters was an old man named John Brown, who thought that God had called him to do all he could for the freedom of the slaves.

Some people think that John Brown was not quite right in his brain. What he did was to gather a body of men and to take possession of Harper's Ferry, on the Potomac River, where there was a government army. He thought that the slaves of Virginia would come to his aid in multitudes and that he could start a slave war that would run all through the South.

It was a wild project. Not a slave came. But some troops came under Colonel Robert E. Lee, and Brown and his party were forced to surrender. Some of them were killed and wounded and the others taken prisoners. John Brown and six others were tried and hanged. But the half-insane old man had done his work. That fight at Harper's Ferry helped greatly to bring on the war.

I said there were two things. The other was the election of Abraham Lincoln as President.

For a long time, as I have told you, the Abolitionists, or people opposed to slavery, were few in number. When they grew more numerous they formed a political party, known as the Anti-slavery Party. In 1856 a new party, called the Republican Party, was formed and took in all the Abolitionists. It was so strong that in the election of that year eleven states voted for its candidate, John C. Fremont, the man who had taken California from Mexico.

In 1860 Abraham Lincoln, a western orator of whom I shall soon tell you more, was the candidate of the Republican Party, and in the election of that year this new party was successful and Lincoln was elected President of the United States.

CHAPTER XXI

HOW LINCOLN BECAME PRESIDENT

I SHOULD like to tell you all about one of the greatest and noblest men who ever lived in our country, and give you his story from the time he was born until the time he died. But that would be biography, and this is a book of history. Biography is the story of a man; history is the story of a nation. So I cannot give you the whole life of Abraham Lincoln, but only that part of it which has to do with the history of our country.

Nations, you should know, are divided into monarchies and republics. In a monarchy the ruler is called a king, or some other name which means the same thing. And when a king dies his son takes his place as king. The king may be noble and wise, or he may be base and foolish; he may be a genius, or he may be an idiot, without any sense at all; he may be kind and just, or he may be cruel and unjust; but for all that he is king. There may be some good points in letting a man be born king, but you can see that there are many bad ones. The history of the nations hasoften shown this, as you may have seen in what we have said of some of the English kings who had to do with America.

In a republic the ruler—who is called president instead of king—is not born to his office, but is chosen by the people; and he cannot rule the nation all his life, but only for a few years. In that way the best and wisest man in the nation may be chosen as its ruler. We do not always get the best man in the United States; but that is the fault of the people, it is not the fault of the plan. There is one thing sure, we never get a fool or an idiot, as kingdoms sometimes do.

There are times when we do choose our best and wisest man, and everybody thinks we did so when we made Abraham Lincoln President. As I have told you, as soon as he was made President a great war began between the two halves of our people. It is not so easy to rule in war as in peace, and I must say that poor Lincoln had a very hard time of it. But he did the best he could, and people say now that no man in our nation could have done better. Abraham Lincoln stands next to George Washington among the great and noble men of America.

There is one more thing it is well to know. It is not only the rich and proud that we choose to be our Presidents. Many of them have begun life as poor boys, and none of them began poorerthan "honest Abe Lincoln," as the people he lived among called him. He well deserved this name, for he was always good and honest.

No doubt there are many poor boys among my readers, but I do not believe that any of you are as poor as was little Abe Lincoln, or have had as hard a life. So you see that while a king must have a king or great noble for father, a President may be the son of the poorest laborer. Any one of my young readers, if he can bring himself strongly to the notice of the people, may become President, and I should not wonder at all if some one among you should do so in future times.

I told you that I would not speak about Abraham Lincoln's early life, but I see that I shall have to do so. He was born in a mean little log-cabin in the back woods a hundred years ago, in the year 1809. His father could not read and did not like to work, and the poor little fellow had hardly enough to eat.

His mother loved him, but she could do little for him, and she died when he was only eight years old. Then his father married a second wife. She was a good woman, and she did all she could for the poor, forlorn little boy. But it did not look much then as if this ragged and hungry little chap would become President of the United States.

There was one good thing about little Abe, hehad a great love for books. He went to school only long enough to learn to read and write, but he borrowed and read all the books he could get. When he found he could not go to school he studied at home. He had no slate or pencil, so he studied arithmetic by the light of the kitchen fire, working out the problems on the back of a wooden fire shovel. When this was full he would scrape it off smooth and begin again. In this way the boy got to be the best scholar in all the country around him. How many of you would have worked as hard as he did to get an education? Yet it was this kind of work that made him President.

Lincoln knew how to make use of his learning. He was always a good talker, and he grew to be one of the best public speakers of his times. He became so well known and so well respected that at length he was sent to Congress. Lincoln did not believe that slavery was a good thing for the country, and was sure it was a wrong thing in itself. So he joined the Republican Party, which had just been formed.

There was another fine speaker in Illinois named Douglas, who had different ideas about slavery from Lincoln and was a member of the Democratic Party. Lincoln and Douglas went about Illinois making speeches to the people, and great crowds came to hear them, for they were two of the best speakers in the country. Everywhere people were talking about Lincoln and Douglas and saying what able men they were.

In 1860 came the time when a new President was to be chosen, and out of all the political leaders of the country these two men from far-west Illinois were selected—Douglas by those who were in favor of slavery and Lincoln by those who opposed slavery. When election day came round and the votes were counted, Abraham Lincoln, the rail splitter, was found to be elected President of the United States.

The people of the South were in a terrible state of mind when they found that a Republican, a man opposed to slavery, was elected President. They could not tell what would take place. The Abolitionists who were against slavery were in power and might pass laws that would rob them of all their slaves. For years they had been fighting the North in Congress—fighting by words, I mean. Now they determined to leave the Union, and to fight with swords and guns if the North would not let them go in peace. One by one the Southern States passed resolutions to go out of the Union. And on all sides they collected powder and balls and other implements of war, for their leaders felt sure they would have to fight. But Lincoln hoped the states would not quarrel. He begged them not to. But if they did it was his duty to do what the people had put him there for. He had been elected President of the United States, and he must do all he could to keep these states united.

It was on the 4th of March, 1861, that Abraham Lincoln became President. By the middle of April the North and South were at war. Both sides had their soldiers in the field and fighting had begun. The South wanted to take Washington, and the North to keep it, and soon a fierce battle was fought at a place called Bull Run, a few miles south of Washington.

The Southern States formed a Union of their own, which was called the Southern Confederacy. They chose Richmond, the capital of Virginia, for the capital of the Confederacy, and chose Jefferson Davis for their President. Davis had fought bravely as a soldier at the battle of Buena Vista, in Mexico. And he had been long in Congress, where he showed himself an able lawmaker. So the South chose him as their best man for President.

The war was half over before President Lincoln did anything about slavery. He was there to save the Union, not to free the slaves. But the time came when he found that freeing the slaves would help him in saving the Union. When this time came—it was on the 1st of January, 1863—he declared that all the slaves should be free. It was a great thing for this country, for it was clear that there could be no peace while slavery remained.

But the war went on more fiercely than ever, and it was not until April, 1865, that it came to an end. The South was not able to fight any longer and had to give up, and the Union was saved. It was saved without slavery, which was a very good thing for both North and South, as we have since found out.

But good and true Abraham Lincoln did not live to learn what the country gained by the war, for just after it ended he was killed by a wicked and foolish man, who thought he would avenge the South by shooting the President.

It was a terrible deed. The whole country mourned for its noblest man, slain in the hour of victory. The South as well as the North suffered by his death, for he was too just a man to oppress those who had been beaten in war, and in him all the people, North and South, lost their best and ablest friend.

CHAPTER XXII

THE GREAT CIVIL WAR

I HAVE no doubt that some of the young folks who read this book will want to hear the story of the great war that was spoken of in the last chapter. Some of the boys will, at any rate. The girls do not care so much about war, and I am glad of this, for I think the world would be much better off if there were no wars.

Well, I suppose I shall have to tell the boys something about it. The girls can skip it, if they wish. To tell the whole story of our Civil War would take a book five times as large as this, so all I can do is to draw a sort of outline map of it. A civil war, you should know, means a war within a nation, where part of a people fight against the other part. A war between two nations is called a foreign war.

When our Civil War broke out we had thirty-three states—we have more than forty-five to-day. Eleven of these states tried to leave the Union and twenty-two remained, so that the Union states were two to one against the non-Union. But the Union states had more than twice the people and had ten times the wealth, so that, as you may see, the war was a one-sided affair. It was nearly all fought in the South, whose people suffered greatly for their attempt to leave the Union. Many of them lost all they had and became very poor.

There were three fields or regions in which this war took place. One of these was a narrow region, lying between Washington and Richmond, the two capital cities. But small as it was, here the greatest battles were fought. Both sides were fighting fiercely to save their capitals.

The second region of the war was in the West. This was a vast region, extending from Kentucky and Missouri down to the Gulf of Mexico. Here there were many long, weary marches and much hard fighting and great loss of life. The third region was on the ocean and rivers, where iron-clad ships first met in battle, and where some famous combats took place.

Over these three regions a million and more of men struggled for years, fighting with rifle and cannon, with sword and bayonet, killing and wounding one another and causing no end of misery in all parts of the land. For the people at home suffered as much as the men on the battle-field, and many mothers and sisters were heartbroken when word came to them that their dear sons or brothers had been shot down on the field of blood.

War is the most terrible thing upon the earth, though men try to make it look like a pleasant show with their banners and trumpets and drums.

As soon as the news of the war came there was a great coming and going of soldiers, and beating of drums, and fluttering of banners, and making of speeches, and thousands marched away, some to Washington and some to Richmond, and many more to the strongholds of the West. Mothers wept as they bade good-by to their sons, whom they might never see again. And many of the soldier-boys had sad hearts under their brave faces. Soon hundreds of these poor fellows were falling dead and wounded on fields of battle, and then their people at home had good reason to weep and mourn.

I have told you about the battle of Bull Run, south of Washington, the first great battle of the war. Here the Southern army gained the victory, and the people of the South were full of joy. But Congress now called for half a million of men and voted half a billion of dollars. Both sides saw that they had a great war before them.

Bull Run was the only severe battle in 1861, but in 1862 both the North and the South had large armies, and there was much hard fighting in the East and the West.

I must tell you first of the fighting in Virginia. General George B. McClellan was in command of the Union army there. He led it down close to Richmond, which he hoped to capture. There was a sharp fight at a place called Fair Oaks, where General Joseph Johnston, the Confederate general, was wounded. General Robert E. Lee took his place. They could not have picked out a better man, for he proved himself to be one of the greatest soldiers of modern times.

The Confederates had another fine general named Thomas J. Jackson. He was called "Stonewall" Jackson, because, in the battle of Bull Run, some one had said:

"Look at Jackson! There he stands like a stone wall!"

General Lee and Stonewall Jackson were not the men to keep quiet. In a short time they drove McClellan back after a hard fight lasting a whole week, and then made a sudden march to the north. Here was another Union army, on the old battle-field of Bull Run. A dreadful battle followed; men fell by thousands; in the end the Union army was defeated and forced back towards Washington.

General Lee knew that he could not take Washington, so he marched away north, waded his men across the Potomac River, and entered the state of Maryland. This was a slave state, and he hoped many of the people would join his army. Butthe farmers of Maryland loved the Union too well for that, so General Lee got very few of them in his ranks.

Then he went west, followed by General McClellan, and at a place called Antietam the two armies met; and there was fought the bloodiest battle of the war. They kept at it all day long and neither side seemed beaten. But that night General Lee and his men waded back across the Potomac into Virginia, leaving McClellan master of the field. There was one more terrible battle in Virginia that year, in which General Burnside, who after McClellan commanded the Union army, tried to take the city of Fredericksburg, but was defeated and his men driven back with a dreadful loss of life.

Both armies now rested until the spring of 1863, and then another desperate battle was fought. General Hooker had taken General Burnside's place, and thought he also must fight a battle, but he did not dare to try Fredericksburg as Burnside had done, so he marched up the river and crossed it into a rough and wild country known as the Wilderness.

General Lee hurried there to meet him and the two armies came together at a place called Chancellorsville. They fought in the wild woods, where the trees in some places were so thick that the men could not see one another. But StonewallJackson marched to the left through the woods and made a sudden attack on the right wing of the Union army.

This part of the army was taken by surprise and driven back. Hooker's men fought all that day and the next, but they could not recover from their surprise and loss, and in the end they had to cross the river back again. General Lee had won another great victory. But Stonewall Jackson was wounded and soon died, and Lee would rather have lost the battle than to lose this famous general.

Do you not think the North had a right to feel very much out of heart by this time? The war had gone on for two years, and the Union army had been defeated in all the great battles fought in Virginia. The only victory won was that at Antietam in Maryland. They had been beaten at the two battles of Bull Run, the seven days' fight at Richmond, and the battles of Fredericksburg and Chancellorsville, while the battle of Antietam had been won with great loss of life.

But there was soon to be a victory that would make up for more than one defeat. Shortly after the fight at Chancellorsville General Lee broke camp and marched north with the greatest speed. The Union army followed as fast as they could march, for there was danger of Baltimore or even Philadelphia being taken. Both armies kept onuntil they reached the town of Gettysburg, in the south of Pennsylvania. Here was fought the greatest battle of the war. It lasted for three days, the 1st, 2d and 3d of July, 1863.

The loss of life on both sides was dreadful. But the Confederates lost the most men and lost the battle besides. They tried in vain to break through the Union lines, and in the end they were forced to retreat. On the 4th of July General Lee sadly began his backward march, and the telegraph wires carried all through the North the tidings of a great victory. This was the turning point in the war. Six months before, President Lincoln had proclaimed the freedom of the slaves, and the armies were now fighting to make his word good. Negroes after this were taken into the Union ranks, that they might help in the fight for their own liberty.

I wish to say just here that the people of the North bore the defeats in Virginia better than you would think. They had good reason to, for while they had been losing battles in the East they had been winning battles in the West. So one helped to make up for the other. If you will follow me now to the West we will see what was taking place there.

The North did not have to change its generals as often in the West as in the East, for it soon found a good one; and it was wise enough to holdon to him. This was General Ulysses S. Grant, who is now honored as one of the greatest generals of the world's history.

Grant was only a captain at first. Then he was made a colonel, and was soon raised to the rank of general. He met the Confederates first at Belmont, Missouri. Here he was defeated, and had to take his men aboard river-boats to get them away. That was his first and nearly his last defeat.

The Confederates had built two strong forts in Kentucky which they named Fort Henry and Fort Donelson. General Grant marched against them with an army and Commodore Foote steamed against them with a fleet of iron-clad steamboats. Fort Henry was taken by the fleet before Grant could get to it. Then he marched across country to Fort Donelson, on the Cumberland River. He attacked this fort so fiercely that the Confederates tried to get out of it but did not succeed. Then they proposed to surrender, and asked him what terms he would give them.

"No terms except an immediate and unconditional surrender," he said. "I propose to move immediately on your works."

This settled the matter. They surrendered—fifteen thousand in all. After that many said that U. S. Grant stood for "Unconditional Surrender" Grant.

I cannot tell you about all the fights that took place in the West, but there was a terrible battle at a place called Pittsburg Landing, which lasted two days, and in which Grant came very near being defeated. There was a severe one at Murfreesboro on the last day of the year, and another three days afterwards. Grant was not there, but Bragg, the Confederate General, was defeated.

The Confederates had an important stronghold on the Mississippi River at the city of Vicksburg, where they had many forts and a large number of cannon. General Sherman tried to capture these forts but was driven back. Then General Grant tried it and found it a very hard task.

The country was all swamp and creeks which no army could get through, so Grant at last marched south on the other side of the river, and then crossed over and marched north again. He had to fight every step of his way, and to live on the food his men could carry, for he had cut loose from the North. But he soon reached the city and began a long siege. The Confederates held out until all their food was gone, and until they had eaten up nearly all their horses and mules. Then they surrendered. Twenty-seven thousand men were taken prisoners.

This took place on the 4th of July, 1863, the same day that General Lee marched away from the field at Gettysburg. That was one of thegreatest Fourths of July this country had ever seen, for with it the last chance of the South was lost. General Lee had lost many thousands of his hardy veterans, men whom he could never replace. And in the fighting around Vicksburg and the capture of that city nearly fifty thousand more fell on the battle-field or were taken prisoners. It was a loss which the leaders of the Southern army bitterly felt. Fighting kept on for two years more, but they would have been wiser to give up then and save all the death and misery that came to them afterwards.

CHAPTER XXIII

WAR ON SEA AND LAND

I HAVE told you part of the story of how our people fought on land. Now suppose we take a look at the water, and see how they fought there. Have any of you heard of the wonderful battle between the "Monitor" and the "Merrimac"? If you have you will be sure to remember it, for it is one of the strangest stories in the history of war. In the lower part of Chesapeake Bay is what I may call a pocket of water named Hampton Roads, into which the James River flows. Here, in the month of March, 1862, lay a fleet of war-vessels. These were not the kind of ships-of-war which we see now-a-days. They were wooden vessels, such as were used in former wars, but which would be of no more use than floating logs against the sea-monsters of to-day.

Something strange was soon to happen to these proud ships. On the 8th of March there came into the waters of the bay a very odd looking craft. It was a ship, but instead of a deck it had a sloping roof made of iron bars. It lookedsomething like a house gone adrift. I fancy the people in the wooden ships must have been a little scared when they saw it coming, for they had never seen a war-vessel with an iron roof before.

They might well be scared, for they soon found that their cannon were of no more use than pea-shooters against this queer craft. The cannon-balls bounded off from her sides like so many peas. On came the monster and struck one of the ships with her iron beak, tearing a great hole in its side. Down into the waters sunk the gallant ship, with all on board. And there it lay with its flag flying like a flag above a grave. Another ship, the "Congress," was driven on the mud and had to give up the fight.

There were three more ships in the fleet, but it was now near night, and so the "Merrimac," as the iron monster was called, steamed away. Her captain thought it would be an easy thing to settle with them the next morning, and very likely the people on them did not sleep well that night, for they could not forget what had happened to the "Congress" and the "Cumberland," and felt sure their turn was to come next.

But, as the old saying goes, "There is many a slip between cup and lip." The "Merrimac" was to learn the truth of this. For when she came grimly out the next day, expecting to sink the rest of the fleet and then steam up to the cityof Washington and perhaps burn that, her captain found before him the queerest thing in the shape of a ship he had ever seen. It was an iron vessel that looked like "a cheese box on a raft." All that could be seen was a flat deck that came just above the water, and above this a round tower of iron, out of which peeped two monsters of cannon.

This strange vessel had come into Hampton Roads during the night, and there it lay ready to do battle for the Union. It was a new style of war-ship that had been built in New York and was called the "Monitor."

The "Merrimac" soon had enough to keep herself busy, and was forced to let the wooden fleet alone. For four long hours these two iron monsters battered each other with cannon balls. Such a fight had never been seen before. It was the first time two iron-clad ships had met in war.

I cannot say that either ship was hurt much. The balls could not get through the iron bars and plates and glanced off into the water. But the "Merrimac" got the worst of it, and in the end she turned and hurried back to Norfolk, from which place she had come. The "Monitor" waited for her, but she never came out again. Soon afterwards the Confederates left Norfolk and sunk their iron ship, and that was the last of the "Merrimac."

When the news of this wonderful sea-fight got to Europe the kings and ministers of war read it with alarm. They saw they had something to do. Their wooden war-vessels were out of date, and they went to work in a hurry to build iron-clad ships. To-day all the great nations of the earth have fleets of steel-covered ships-of-war, and the United States has some of the best and strongest of this kind of ships.

All through the war there were battles of iron-clads. On the western rivers steamboats were plated with iron and attacked the forts on shore. And along the coast iron-clad vessels helped the wooden ships to blockade the ports of the South. More vessels like the "Monitor" were built in the North, and a number somewhat like the "Merrimac" were built in the South. I cannot say that any of them did much good either North or South.

A great naval battle was fought in the Mississippi, which led to the capture of New Orleans, and another was fought in the Bay of Mobile, on the Gulf of Mexico. Here there were some strong forts and a powerful iron-clad ship. Admiral Farragut sailed into the bay with a fleet of wooden ships and several iron vessels like the "Monitor." When he went past the forts he stood in the rigging of his ship, with his spy-glass in his hand. He did not seem to care anything for cannon-balls.He took the forts, and since then Farragut has been one of our great naval heroes.

There was one Confederate privateer, the "Alabama," which caused terrible loss to the merchants of the North. It took in all sixty-five vessels, which were set on fire and burned. In June, 1864, the "Alabama" was met near the coast of France by the frigate "Kearsarge," and a furious battle took place.

For two hours they fought, and then the "Alabama" sagged down into the water and sank to the bottom of the sea. She had done much harm to the North, but her career was at an end.

Now let us turn back to the war on land and see what was going on there. I have told you the story of the fighting up to the great 4th of July, 1863, when Vicksburg surrendered to General Grant and General Lee marched away from Gettysburg. That is where we dropped the threads which we have now to take up again.

After Grant had taken Vicksburg and opened the Mississippi from St. Louis to its mouth, he set out for the town of Chattanooga, which is in Tennessee just north of Georgia. Here there had been a great battle in which the Confederate army won the victory, and the Union troops were shut up in Chattanooga with very little to eat.

Grant was not there long before there came a change. General Bragg, the Confederate commander,had his army on the summits of two mountains named Lookout Mountain and Missionary Ridge. These were defended by strong forts. But the Union troops charged up the mountain sides in the face of the fire of rifles and cannon and soon had possession of the forts. General Bragg's army was defeated with great loss. This was one of the most brilliant victories of the war. The battle of Lookout Mountain has been called "the battle above the clouds."

Everybody now saw that General Grant was much the best general on the Union side, and President Lincoln made him commander-in-chief of all the armies in the field. Grant at once laid his plans to have the armies all work together. General Sherman was left in command of the army of the West and Grant came to Virginia to fight General Lee.

In the green month of May, 1864, all the armies were set in motion, and North and South came together for the last great struggle of the war.

Grant led his men into the Wilderness where General Hooker and his army had been sadly defeated the year before. Lee was there to meet him, and a great battle was fought in the depth of the woods and thickets. It lasted two whole days, but neither side won.

Then Grant marched towards Richmond and Lee hurried down to head him off. Several hardbattles were fought, the last being at Cold Harbor, near Richmond. Here the Union army lost terribly. Ten thousand men were killed and wounded, while the Confederates, who were behind strong earthworks, lost only a thousand.

General Grant saw he could not reach Richmond that way, so he crossed the James River and began a siege of Petersburg and Richmond. This siege lasted nine months, both sides digging instead of fighting till great heaps of earth were thrown up, on whose tops were hundreds of cannon.

General Grant kept his men very busy, as you may see. But General Sherman's men were just as busy. He marched south from Chattanooga, and fought battle after battle until he had gone far into Georgia and captured the important city of Atlanta. General Hood, the Confederate commander, then made a rapid march to Tennessee, thinking that Sherman would follow him. But Sherman did not move. The brave General Thomas was there to take care of Hood and his army.

"Let him go; he couldn't please me better," said Sherman.

What Sherman did was to cut loose from the railroads and telegraphs and march his whole army into the center of Georgia. For a whole month the people of the North heard nothing of him. His sixty thousand men might be starvingfor food, or might all be killed, so far as was known. It was November when they started and it was near Christmas when they were heard of again.

They had lived on the country and destroyed railroads and stores, and at length they came to the sea at the city of Savannah. Three daring scouts made their way in a boat down the river by night and brought to the fleet the first news of Sherman's march. No doubt you have heard the song "Marching through Georgia." That was written to describe Sherman's famous march.

The South was now getting weaker, and weaker, and most men saw that the war was near its end. It came to an end in April, 1865. Grant kept moving south till he got round the Confederate earthworks at Petersburg, and Lee was forced to leave Richmond in great haste.

The Union army followed as fast as it could march, and the cavalry rode on until it was ahead of the Confederates. Then General Lee saw that he was surrounded by an army far stronger than his own. He could fight no longer. His men were nearly starved. To fight would be to have them all killed. So on the 9th of April he offered his sword to General Grant, and the long and bloody war was at an end.

No one was gladder of this than President Lincoln, who had done so much to bring it about.Poor man! five days afterwards he was shot in a theatre at Washington by an actor named John Wilkes Booth. This was done out of revenge for the defeat of the South. But the people of the South did not approve of this act of murder, and in Abraham Lincoln they lost one whom they would have found a good friend.

Booth was followed and killed, but his death could not bring back to life the murdered President, whom the people loved so warmly that they mourned for him as if he had been, like Washington, the Father of his Country. It was a terrible crime, and it turned the joy which the people felt, at the end of the war, into the deepest sorrow and grief.

CHAPTER XXIV

THE WASTE OF WAR AND THE WEALTH OF PEACE

LET us suppose that the history of the whole world is spread out before us like a picture, and that we are looking down on it. What will we see? Well, we will see places where a terrible storm seems to have swept over the picture, and left only darkness and ruin in its track. And we will see other places where the sun seems to have poured down its bright beams, and all is clear and bright and beautiful. The dark places are those of war; the bright places are those of peace. All through history there have been times when men have gone out to kill and burn and do all the harm they could; and there have been other times when they stayed at home to work, and build up what war had cast down, and bring plenty and happiness to the nations.

In the picture of our own history we see such dark and bright places. And the darkest of them all is the terrible Civil War, the story of which you have just read. For in this war our people fought against and killed one another, and all the harmwas done at home, instead of in foreign lands. The war was a dreadful one. Hundreds of thousands of our people were killed or wounded, and the ground in hundreds of places was red with blood. Houses, barns and factories were burned, railroads were torn up, ships were sunk, growing crops were trampled into the earth. And last of all came that horrid murder of our good and great President Lincoln, one of the best and noblest men who ever sat in the presidential chair. Such is war—the most frightful thing we can think of or talk about. Some of my young friends may like to play soldier; but if they should grow up and get to be real soldiers they would find out what war means. Now, if we look again at the picture of our history, we shall see a great bright space of peace following the dark space of the Civil War. That is what I wish to tell you about now—the reign of peace, when everybody was busy at work in building up what had been torn down by the red hand of war, and our country grew faster than it had ever grown before.

There is one thing I must say here. I have told you that slavery was the cause of the war. If there had been no slaves in the country there would have been no war. And the one good thing the war did for us was to get rid of the slaves. President Lincoln declared that all the slaves should be free, and since that time there has notbeen a slave in the land. So we can never have a war for that cause again.

When the war was done, the soldiers marched back to their homes. Their old battle-flags, rent and torn by bullets, were put away as valued treasures; their rusty rifles, which had killed thousands of men, were given back to the government; they took up their axes, they went into the fields with their ploughs, they entered the workshops with their tools, and soon they were all at work again, as if they had never seen a field of battle.

This took place long before any of my young readers were born. But there are many old soldiers living who took part in it, and when you see the veterans of the Grand Army of the Republic, marching with their ragged flags and battle-scarred faces, it may bring to you some vision of what they have seen, and make you think of the fallen comrades they left behind, dead or bleeding upon the battle-field.

During your short lives there has been no war which came near to us in our homes. The angel of peace has spread her white wings over our land, and plenty and prosperity have been the rule. None of our young folks have known what it is for an army of soldiers to march past their homes, destroying and burning, and leaving ashes and ruins where there had been happy homes and fertile fields. But in the past of our country thishappened to many as young as you, and they were glad that their lives were left them, after everything else was gone.

Let us put the thought of war out of our minds, and go on to see what took place under the blessed reign of peace. The first thing of which I shall tell you was one of the most wonderful of all. You know how the telegraph wires spread over the country until they were many thousands of miles in length. In the next chapter you may read how the electric telegraph was invented. In the year after the war ended a still greater thing was done. A telegraph cable was laid under the ocean from Europe to America. This had been done before, but it had proved a failure. The new cable was a success, and since then a man in London has been able to talk with a man in New York as if he were not a hundred yards away. Of course, I do not mean with his voice, but with the click of the telegraph instrument.

The year after that a great addition was made to the United States. There was a large region in the north, known as Russian America, which Russia offered to sell to this country for seven million dollars. Many people talked about this as some of their forefathers had talked about the purchase of Louisiana by President Jefferson. They said that it was a land of ice and snow which Russia wanted to get rid of, and that it would beof no use to anybody. But it was bought for all that, and it has proven a very good bargain.

This country we now call Alaska. We get there all the sealskins from which the rich and warm cloaks of the ladies are made. And most of the canned salmon, which some of you think very good food, come from Alaska. That country is rich in furs and fish and timber; and that is not all, for it is rich in gold. Millions of dollars worth of gold are obtained there every year. It has been something like California, whose gold was not found till Americans got there to dig.

These are not the only things that took place in the years after the war. Railroads were being built in all directions. East and west, north and south, they went, and travel became easier than it had been before. The greatest thing done in this way was the building of a railroad across the mountains and the plains to San Francisco, on the far Pacific coast, three thousand miles away from the Atlantic shores. Before that time men who wanted to go to California had to drag along over thousands of miles in slow wagon trains and spend weeks and months on the road. Now they could go there in less than a week. It was the longest railroad that the world had ever seen, up to that time.

While all this was going on, people were comingto this country in great multitudes, crossing the ocean to find new homes in our happy land. They did not have to come in slow sailing ships as in former times, but were brought here in swift steamships, that crossed the seas almost as fast as the iron horse crossed the land. All these new people went to work, some in the cities and some in the country, and they all helped to make our nation rich and powerful.

But you must not think that everything went well, and that we had no dark days. Every country has its troubles, even in times of peace. War is not the only trouble. Great fires break out, storms sweep over the land, earthquakes shake down cities, and many other disasters take place. Of all these things, fire, when it gets beyond control, is the most terrible; and it is of a frightful fire that I wish to speak.

About the year 1831 a small fort stood near the shore of Lake Michigan, and around this a few pioneer families had built their homes, which were only rude log houses. In 1871, forty years afterwards, the fort and the huts had long been gone and a large city stood at that place. Its growth had been wonderful. Only forty years old and already it was one of the great cities of the country. This was the famous city of Chicago, which has grown more rapidly than any other great city ever known.

One night in October a dreadful thing took place in this city. A cow kicked over a lamp in a stable. The straw on the floor took fire, and in a minute the blaze shot up into the air. The people ran for water, but they were too slow, and in a few minutes the whole stable was in flames. You may think that this was not of much account, but there happened to be a gale of wind, and soon great blazing fragments were flying through the air and falling on roofs squares away. It was not long before there was a terrible fire over almost the entire city.

Chicago at that time was mostly built of wood, and the fire spread until it looked as if the whole great city would be burnt to ashes. For two days it kept on burning until the richest part of the city had gone up in smoke and flame. Many people were burned to death in the streets and two hundred million dollars worth of property was destroyed. It was the most frightful fire of modern times. But Americans do not stop for fire or water. The city was built up again, far handsomer than before, and it is now one of the greatest cities, not only of this country, but of the world.

This was not the only disaster which came upon the country. In 1886 there was a frightful earthquake in South Carolina, that shook down a great part of the city of Charleston. And in 1889 therewas a terrible flood that swept away the young city of Johnstown, in Pennsylvania, and drowned more than two thousand people. And there were tornadoes, or wind storms, in the west that blew down whole towns as you might blow down a house of cardboard with your breath. And there were great strikes and riots that were almost like war, and various other troubles. But all these could not stop the growth of the country. Every year it became richer. New people came, new factories were built, new fields were farmed, and the United States seemed like a great hive of industry, and its people like so many bees, working away, day by day, and gathering wealth as bees gather honey.

It not only got many of the old articles of wealth, but it found many new ones also. Never was there a country with so many inventors or men that have made things new and useful to everybody, and never were there more wonderful inventions. I have told you about some of our inventors; I shall have to speak of some more of them. There were hundreds of men busily at work at inventing new machines and tools, new things to help everybody—the farmer, the merchant, the workman in the factory, and the cook in the kitchen. It went on so that there was not much done by hand, as in old times, but nearly everything was done by machine.

CHAPTER XXV

THE MARVELS OF INVENTION

IT is not a pleasant thing to go hungry for twenty-four hours and to go many days without half enough to eat. I think all my readers will agree with me in this. I fancy none of you would like to find an empty table before you when the dinner bell rings. But this is a thing that has happened to many inventors; and one of these was Samuel F. B. Morse, to whose genius we owe the electric telegraph.

THE WRIGHT BROTHERS AND THEIR FAMOUS AEROPLANE.

You know about the invention of the steamboat, the locomotive, the cotton-gin and various other early inventions; but there have been many later inventions, and one of the most important of these is the telegraph, which tells us every day what is taking place over the whole world.

Professor Morse was a New York artist who studied painting in Europe, and in the year 1832 took passage home in the ship "Sully." One day a talk went on in the cabin of the ship. Dr. Jackson, one of the passengers, told how some persons in Paris had sent an electric current through several miles of wire in less than a second of time.

"If that is the case," said Morse, "why could not words and sentences be sent in the same way?"

"That's a good idea. It would be a great thing if we could send news as fast as lightning," said one of the passengers.

"Why can't we?" said Morse; "I think we can do it."

Very likely the rest of the passengers soon forgot all about that conversation, but Morse did not. During the remainder of the voyage he was very quiet and kept much to himself. He was thinking over what he had heard. Before the ship had reached New York he had worked out a plan of telegraphing. He proposed to carry the wire in tubes underground, and to use an alphabet of dots and dashes, the same that is used by telegraphers to-day.

When he went on shore Morse said to the captain: "Captain, if you should hear of the telegraph one of these days as the wonder of the world, remember that the discovery was made on board the good ship 'Sully.'"

"If I can make it go ten miles without stopping, I can make it go round the world," he said to a passenger.

But it is easier to think out a thing than to put it in practice. Poor Morse was more than ten years in working out his plans and getting people to help him in them. He got out of money andwas near starving, but he kept at it. After three years he managed to send a message through seventeen hundred feet of wire. He could read it, but his friends could not, and no one was ready to put money in such a scheme. They looked at it as a toy to amuse children. Then he went to Europe and tried to get money there, but he found the people there as hard to convince as those in America.

"No one is in such a hurry for news as all that," they said. "People would rather get their news in the good old way. Your wires work, Mr. Morse, but it would take a great deal of money to lay miles of them underground, and we are not going to take such chances as that with our money."

Mr. Morse next tried to get Congress to grant him a sum of money. He wanted to build a wire from Baltimore to Washington and show how it would work. But it is never easy to get money from Congress, and he kept at it for five years in vain.

It was the 3d of March, 1843. At twelve o'clock that night the session of Congress would end. Morse kept about the Senate chamber till nearly midnight, in hopes his bill would pass. Then he gave it up in despair and went to his boarding house. He was sure his little bill would not be thought of in the crowd of business beforeCongress and was greatly depressed in consequence.

He came down to breakfast the next morning with a very sad face, hardly knowing how he was to pay his board and get home. He was met by a young lady, Miss Annie Ellsworth, who came to him with a smile.

"Let me congratulate you, Mr. Morse," she said.

"For what, my dear friend?"

"For the passage of your bill."

"What!" he said, in great astonishment; "the passage of my bill?"

"Yes; do you not know of it?"

"No; it cannot be true!"

"You came home too early last night, Mr. Morse. Your bill has passed, and I am happy to be the first to bring you the good news."

"You give me new life, Miss Ellsworth," he said. "For your good news I promise you this: when my telegraph line is laid, you shall have the honor of selecting the first message to be sent over it."

Congress had granted only thirty thousand dollars. It was not much, but Morse went actively to work. He wanted to dig a ditch to lay his pipe in, through which the wire was to run. He got another inventor to help him, Ezra Cornell,who afterwards founded Cornell University. Mr. Cornell invented a machine which dug the ditch at a great rate, laid the pipe, and covered it in. In five minutes it laid and covered one hundred feet of pipe.

But Cornell did not think the underground wire would work.

"It will work," said Morse. "While I have been fighting Congress, men have laid short lines in England which work very well. What can be done there can be done here."

For all that, it would not work. A year passed and only seven thousand dollars of the money were left, and all the wires laid were of no use.

"If it won't go underground we must try and coax it to go over-ground," said Morse.

Poles were erected; the wire was strung on glass insulators; it now worked to a charm. On May 11, 1844, the Whig National Convention at Baltimore nominated Henry Clay for President, and the news was sent to Washington in all haste by the first railroad train. But the passengers were surprised to find that they brought stale news; everybody in Washington knew it already. It had reached there an hour or two before by telegraph. That was a great triumph for Morse. The telegraph line was not then finished quite to Baltimore. When it reached there, on May24th, the first message sent was one which Miss Ellsworth had chosen from the Bible, "What hath God wrought?" God had wrought wonderfully indeed, for since then the electric wire has bound the ends of the earth together.

If I should attempt to tell you about all our inventors I am afraid it would be a long story. There is almost no end to them, and many of them invented wonderful machines. I might tell you, for instance, about Thomas

Blanchard, who invented the machine by which tacks are made, dropping them down as fast as a watch can tick. This is only one out of many of his inventions. One of them was a steamboat to run in shallow water, and which could go hundreds of miles up rivers where Fulton's steamboat would have run aground.

Then there was Cyrus McCormick, who invented the reaping machine. When he showed his reaper at the London World's Fair in 1851, the newspapers made great fun of it. The London "Times" said it was a cross between a chariot, a wheelbarrow and a flying-machine. But when it was put in a wheat-field and gathered in the wheat like a living and thinking machine, they changed their tune, and the "Times" said it was worth more than all the rest of the Exhibition. This was the first of the great agriculturalmachines. Since then hundreds have been made, and the old-fashioned slow hand-work in the fields is over. McCormick made a fortune out of his machine. I cannot say that of all inventors, for many of them had as hard a time as Morse with his telegraph. Two of them, Charles Goodyear and Elias Howe, came as near starving as Professor Morse.

All the rubber goods we have to-day we owe to Charles Goodyear. Before his time India-rubber was of very little use. It would grow stiff in the winter and sticky in the summer, and people said it was a nuisance. What was wanted was a rubber that would stand heat and cold, and this Goodyear set himself to make.

After a time he tried mixing sulphur with the gum, and by accident touched a red-hot stove with the mixture. To his delight the gum did not melt. Here was the secret. Rubber mixed with sulphur and exposed to heat would stand heat and cold alike. He had made his discovery, but it took him six years more to make it a success, and he never made much money from it. Yet everybody honors him to-day as a great inventor.

Elias Howe had as hard a time with the sewing machine. For years he worked at it, and when he finished it nobody would buy it or use it. He went to London, as Morse had done, and had the same bad luck. He had to pawn his modeland patent papers to get home again. His wife was very sick, and he reached home only in time to see her die.

Poor fellow! life was very dark to him then. His invention had been stolen by others, who were making fortunes out of it while he was in need of bread. Friends lent him money and he brought suit against these robbers, but it took six years to win his rights in the courts. In the end he grew rich and gained great honor from his invention.

There has been no man more talked of in our time than Thomas A. Edison. All of you must have heard of him. He went into business when he was only twelve years old, selling newspapers and other things on the cars, and he was so bright and did so well that he was able to send his parents five hundred dollars a year. When he was sixteen he saved the child of a station-master from being run over by a locomotive, and the father was so grateful that he taught him how to telegraph. He was so quick in his work that he become one of the best telegraph operators in the United States.

After he grew up Edison began to invent. He worked out a plan by which he could send two messages at once over one wire. He kept at this till he could send sixteen messages over a wire, eight one way and eight the other. He made money out of his inventions, but the telegraphcompanies made much more. Instead of sending fifty or sixty words a minute, he showed them how they could send several thousand words a minute.

Then he began experimenting with the electric light. He did not invent this, but he made great improvements in it. The electric light could be made, but it could not be controlled and used before Edison taught people how to keep it in its little glass bulb. How brilliantly the streets, the stores, and many of the houses are now lit up by electricity. All from Edison's wonderful discoveries.

Then there was the telephone, or talking telegraph, which many of you may have used yourselves. That was not known before 1876; but people now wonder how they ever got along without it. It is certainly very wonderful, when you have to speak with somebody a mile or a hundred miles away, to ring him up and talk with him over the telephone wire as easily as if you were talking with some one in the next room. The telephone, as I suppose you know, works by electricity. It is only another form of the telegraph. The telephone was not invented by Edison, but by another American named Alexander Bell. But Edison improved it. He added the "transmitter," which is used in all telephones, and is very important indeed. So we must give credit first to Bell and second to Edison for the telephone.

Edison's most wonderful invention is the phonograph. This word means "sound writer." One of you may talk with a little machine, and the sound of your voice will make marks on a little roll of gelatine or tinfoil within. Then when the machine is set going you may hear your own voice coming back to you. Or by the use of a great trumpet called a megaphone, it may be heard all over a large room.

The wonderful thing is that the sound of a man's voice may be heard long after he is dead. If they had possessed the phonograph in old times we might be able to hear Shakespeare or Julius Cæsar speaking to-day. Very likely many persons who live a hundred or two hundred years from now may hear Edison's voice coming out of one of his own machines. Does not this seem like magic?

In every way this is a wonderful age of invention. Look at the trolley car, shooting along without any one being able to see what makes it move. Look at the wheels whirling and lights flashing and stoves heating from electric power. Steam was the most powerful thing which man knew a century ago. Electricity has taken its place as the most powerful and marvelous thing we know to-day. More wonderful than anything I have said is the power we now have of telegraphing without wires, and of telephoning in the same way. Thus men can now stand on the shore and talk withtheir friends hundreds of miles away on the broad sea.

Such are some of the inventions which have been made in recent times. If you ask for more I might name the steam plow, and the typewriter, and the printing machine, and the bicycle, and the automobile, and the air-ship, and a hundred others. But they are too many for me to say anything about, so I shall have to stop right here.

CHAPTER XXVI

HOW THE CENTURY ENDED FOR THE UNITED STATES

VERY likely many of my young readers live in the city of Philadelphia, which was founded by William Penn more than two hundred years ago on the banks of the broad Delaware River, and where now many more than a million people make their homes. And many of you who do not live there, but who love your country and are proud of its history, are likely to go there some time during your lives, to visit the birthplace of your noble nation.

Have you ever thought that the United States, as an independent nation, was born in Philadelphia? In that city stands the stately Independence Hall, in which the Declaration of Independence was made and signed. You may see there the famous old bell, which rang out "Liberty throughout the land!" And you may stand in the room in which our grand Constitution was formed. So Philadelphia should be a place of pilgrimage to all true-hearted Americans, who wish to see where their country was born.

It was such a place of pilgrimage in the year 1876. Then from every part of our country, from the North, the South, the West and the East, our people made their way in thousands towards that great city, which was then the proud center of all American thought. A hundred years had passed from the time the famous Declaration was signed, and the Centennial Anniversary which marked the one hundredth year after this great event was being celebrated in the city which may be called the cradle of the American nation.

A grand exhibition was held. It was called a "World's Fair," for splendid objects were sent to it from all parts of the world, and our own country sent the best of everything it had to show, from Maine to California. On the broad lawns of Fairmount Park many handsome buildings were erected, all filled with objects of use or beauty, and more than ten million people passed through the gates, glad to see what America and the world had to show.

If you wish to know what our own country showed, I may say that the most striking things were its inventions, machines that could do almost everything which the world wants done. And the newest and most wonderful of all these things was the telephone. This magical invention was shown there to the people for the firsttime, and the first voice shouted "Hallo!" over the talking wire.

In the years that followed centennial celebrations became common. In 1881 the centennial anniversary of the surrender of Cornwallis was celebrated at Yorktown. In 1882 the bi-centennial (the two hundredth anniversary) of the landing of William Penn was celebrated at Philadelphia. A vessel that stood for the old ship "Welcome" sailed up the stream, and a man dressed like the famous old Quaker landed and was greeted by a number of men who took the part of Indian chiefs.

In 1887 Philadelphia had another grand anniversary, that of the signing of the Constitution of the United States, which was celebrated by magnificent parades and processions, while the whole city was dressed in the red, white and blue. In 1889 New York celebrated the next grand event in the history of the nation, the taking of the oath by Washington, our first President.

The next great anniversary was that of the discovery of America by Columbus, four hundred years before. This was celebrated by a wonderfully splendid exhibition at Chicago, the most beautiful that the world had ever seen. Columbus landed in October, 1492, and the buildings were dedicated in October, 1892, but the exhibition did not take place till the next year. Those who sawthis exhibition will never forget it, and very likely some of my readers were among them. Its buildings were like fairy palaces, so white and grand and beautiful; and at night, when it was lit up by thousands of electric lights, the whole place looked like fairy land. The world will not soon see anything more beautiful.

I cannot tell of all the exhibitions. There were others, at New Orleans, Atlanta, and other cities, but I think you will be satisfied with hearing about the large ones. The Centennial at Philadelphia set the fashion. After that, cities all over the country wanted to have their great fairs, and many of the little towns had their centennial celebrations, with music and parades, speeches and fireworks.

During all this time the country kept growing. People crossed the ocean in millions. Our population went up, not like a tree growing, but like a deer jumping. In 1880 we had 50,000,000 people. In 1900 we had half as many more. Just think of that! Over 25,000,000 people added in twenty years! How many do you think we will have when the youngest readers of this book get to be old men and women? I am afraid to guess.

As our people increased in number they spread more widely over the country. Railroads were built everywhere, steamboats ran on all thestreams, telegraphs and telephones came near to every man's front door, the post-offices spread until letters and newspapers and packages were carried to the smallest village in the land. Nobody wanted to stay at home, in the old fashion. People thought nothing of a journey across the continent or the ocean. Wherever they were, they could talk with their friends by letter or telegraph, and they could go nowhere that the newspaper could not follow them.

So the waste places of the country began rapidly to fill up. If you have ever seen an old-time map of our country you must have noticed places in the West marked "great desert," or "unknown territory," or by some such name. But people made their way into these unknown regions and filled them up. First they went with their families and household goods in great wagons. Then they went far more swiftly in railroad trains. Here they settled down and began farming; farther on, where there was not rain enough to farm, they raised cattle and sheep on the rich grasses; still farther, in the mountain regions, they set to work mining, getting gold, silver, copper, iron and coal from the hard rocks.

Cities grew up where the Indian and the buffalo had roamed. The factory followed the farmer; the engine began to puff its steam into the air, the wheels to turn, the machines to work, goods of allkinds to be made. The whole country became like a great hive of workers, where everybody was busy, and thousands of the people grew rich.

CUSTER'S LAST FIGHT.

But all this great western country was not given up to the farmer, the miner and the wood-chopper. There were places which nature had made beautiful or wonderful or grand, and these were kept as places for all the people to visit. One of these was the beautiful Yosemite Valley, in California; another was the wonderful Yellowstone Park, with its marvelous spouting springs; others were the groves of giant trees; still others were great forests, from which the government told the wood-choppers to keep out, for the woods had been set aside for the good or the pleasure of all the people of the land.

Some of you may ask, what became of the old people of the country—the Indians, who were spread all over the West? There were hundreds of tribes of them, and many of them were bold and brave, and when they saw the white men pushing into their country they fought fiercely for their homes. But they could not stand before the guns of the pioneers and the cannon of the soldiers, and in time they were all forced to submit. Then places were set aside for them and they were made to live in them. The Indians were not always treated well. They were robbed and cheated in a hundred ways. But that, I hope, is all overnow, for they are being well cared for and educated, and they seem likely, before many years, to become good and useful citizens of our country.

Now I have another story to tell. Our Civil War, which you have read about, ended in 1865. For thirty-three years after that—one-third of a century—we were at peace at home and abroad, and our country had the wonderful growth of which you have just read. Then, in 1898, almost at the end of the century, war came again. By good luck, it was not a big war this time, and it was one I can tell you about in a few words.

It was pity and charity that brought us into this war. South of Florida is the large and fertile island of Cuba, which had long belonged to Spain, and whose people had been very badly treated. At length they said they could stand it no longer, so they took their guns, left their homes, and went to war with the soldiers of Spain. For two years they fought bravely. Their old men, and their women and children, who had stayed at home, helped them all they could; so the Spaniards drove these from their homes into the cities, and left them there with hardly anything to eat. Thousands of these poor wretches starved to death.

You may be sure that our people thought this very wicked. They said that it ought to be stopped; but Spain would not do what they wished. Then they sent food to the starving people. Someof it got to them and some of it was used by others. Everybody in our country felt very badly to see this terrible affair going on at our very doors, and the government was told that it ought to take some action. What the government did was to send one of its war-vessels, the "Maine," to the harbor of Havana, the capital of Cuba.

Then something took place that would have made almost any country go to war. One dark night, while the "Maine" floated on the waters of the harbor, and nearly all her crew were fast asleep in their berths, a terrible explosion was heard under her, and the good vessel was torn nearly in half. In a minute she sank into the muddy bottom of the harbor, and hundreds of her sleeping crew were drowned. Only the captain and some of the officers and men escaped alive.

I fancy all of you must know how angry our people felt when they heard of this dreadful event. You were angry yourselves, no doubt, and said that the Spaniards had done this and ought to be punished by having Cuba taken from them. I do not think there were many Americans who did not feel like taking revenge for our poor murdered sailors.

War soon came. In April, 1898, the Congress declared war against Spain and a strong fleet of iron-clad ships was sent to Cuba. An army was gathered as quickly as possible, and the soldierswere put on board ship and sailed away to the south. There was a Spanish fleet in the harbor of Santiago de Cuba and an American fleet outside keeping the ships of Spain like prisoners in the harbor; so the soldiers were sent to that place, and it was not long before an army was landed and was marching towards the city of Santiago. I am glad to say that the fighting did not last very long. There was a bold charge up hill by the Rough Riders and others in the face of the Spanish guns, and the Spanish army was driven back to the city. Here they were shut up and soon surrendered, and the war in Cuba was at an end.

But the iron-clad ships in the harbor were not given up. On the 3d of July a brave dash for liberty was made. They came out at full speed where our great ships lay waiting, and soon there was one of the strangest fights that had ever been seen. The Spanish ships rushed through the waters near the coast, firing as they fled. After them came the American ships at full speed, firing as they followed. But not many of the Spanish halls touched the American ships, while the great guns of the Americans raked the Spaniards fore and aft.

Soon some of their ships were on fire and had to be run ashore. In an hour or two the chase was at an end and the fine Spanish fleet was sunk and burning, with hundreds of its crew killed, whileon the American ships only one man had been killed. It was a wonderful flight and fight. I should tell you more about it, only that I have another story of the same kind to relate.

Far away from Cuba, on the other side of the world, in the broad Pacific Ocean, near the coast of China, is a great group of islands called the Philippines, which had long belonged to Spain. Here, in the harbor of Manila, the capital of the islands, was a Spanish fleet. There was an American fleet in one of the harbors of China, under the command of Commodore George Dewey. And as soon as war had been declared Dewey was ordered to go to Manila and sink or take the Spanish fleet.

Dewey was a man who thought it his duty to obey orders. He had been told to sink or take the Spanish fleet, and that was what he meant to try his best to do. Over the waters sped his ships, as swiftly as steam could carry them, and into the harbor of Manila they went at midnight while deep darkness lay upon the waters. It was early morning of the 1st of May when the American ships rounded up in front of the city and came in sight of the Spanish fleet. This lay across the mouth of a little bay with forts to guard it on the land at each side.

It was a great danger which Commodore Dewey and his bold followers faced. Beforethem lay the Spanish ships and the forts. There were torpedo boats which might rush out and sink them. There were torpedoes under the waters which might send the flagship itself to the bottom. Some men would have stopped and felt their way, but George Dewey was not that kind of a man. Without stopping for a minute after his long journey from China, he dashed on with the fleet and ordered his men to fire. Soon the great guns were roaring and the air was full of fire and smoke.

Round and round went the American ships, firing as they passed. Every shot seemed to tell. It was not long before some of the Spanish ships were blazing, while hardly a ball had touched an American hull. After an hour or two of this hot work Dewey drew out and gave his men their breakfast. Then back he came and finished the job. When he was done, the whole Spanish fleet was sunk and burning, with hundreds of its men dead and wounded, while not an American ship was badly hurt and not an American sailor was killed. There had hardly been so one-sided a battle since the world began.

There, I have, as I promised, told you in few words the story of the war. Soon after a treaty of peace was signed and all was at an end. The brave Dewey was made an admiral and was greatly honored by the American people.

If you should ask me what we gained from the war, I would answer that we gained in the first place what the war was fought for, the freedom of Cuba from the cruel rule of Spain. But we did not come out of it without something for ourselves. We obtained the fertile island of Porto Rico in the West Indies and the large group of the Philippine Islands, near the coast of Asia. These last named came as the prize of Dewey's victory, but I am sorry to say that there was a war with the people themselves before the United States got possession. During the war with Spain we obtained another fine group of islands, that known as Hawaii, in the Pacific Ocean. You can see from this that our country made a wide spread over the seas at the end of the nineteenth century. The winning of all these islands was an event of the greatest importance to the United States. It gave this country a broad foothold on the seas and a new outlook over the earth. Some of the proud nations of Europe had looked on this country as an American power only, with no voice in world affairs. But when Uncle Sam set his left foot on the Hawaiian Islands, in the Central Pacific, and his right foot on the Philippine Islands, near the coast of Asia, these powers of Europe opened their eyes and began to get new ideas about the great republic of the West. It was plain that the United States had become a world power, andthat when the game of empire was to be played the western giant must be asked to take a hand.

This was seen soon after, when China began to murder missionaries and try to drive all white people from its soil. For the first time in history the United States joined hands with Europe in an Old World quarrel, and it was made evident that the world could not be cut up and divided among the powers without asking permission from Uncle Sam. But fortunately Uncle Sam wants to keep out of war.

And now we are near the end of our long journey. We have traveled together for more than four hundred years, from the time of Columbus to the present day, looking at the interesting facts of our country's history, and following its growth from a tiny seed planted in the wilderness to a giant tree whose branches are beginning to overshadow the earth. We have read about what our fathers did in the times that are no more. We have learned something of what has been taking place during our own lives. There is a new history before us in which we shall live and act and of which our own doings will form part. A new century, the twentieth, has opened before us, and it only remains to tell what our country has done in the few years that have passed of this century.

CHAPTER XXVII

HOW A HUNTER BECAME PRESIDENT

I THINK it very likely that all, or nearly all, who read this book were born before the new century—the one we call the twentieth—began. It is a young century still. Yet there has been time enough for many things to take place in the country we call our own. Some of these you may remember. Others many of you were too young to know much about. So it is my purpose here to bring the story of our country up to the present time.

ROOSEVELT SURPRISED BY A GIANT HIPPOPOTAMUS.

I have not said much about our Presidents, but there was a President elected in the first year of the twentieth century of whom I must speak, since his election led to a dreadful event. In the following year (1901) a beautiful exhibition was held at Buffalo, New York. It was called the Pan American Exhibition, and was intended to show what the nations of America had done in the century just closed.

I shall say little about the splendid electrical display, the fountains with their colored lights, the shining cascades, the glittering domes and pinnacles,the caverns and grottoes, and all the other brilliant things to be seen, for I have to speak of something much less pleasant, the dark deed of murder and treachery which took place at this exhibition.

President McKinley came to Buffalo early in September to see the fine display and let the people see him, and on the 6th he stood with smiling face while many hundreds of visitors passed by and shook hands with him. In the midst of all this there came a loud, sharp sound. A pistol had been fired. The President staggered back, with pallid face. Men shouted; women screamed; a crowd rushed towards the spot; the man who held the pistol was flung to the floor and hundreds surged forward in fury. "He has shot our President! Kill him! Kill him!" they cried. The guards had a hard fight to keep the murderer from being torn to pieces by the furious throng.

The man who had shot the President belonged to a society called Anarchists, who hate all rulers and think it their duty to kill all kings and presidents. Poor, miserable wretch! he suffered the death he deserved. But his shot had reached its mark, and after a week of fear and hope, President McKinley died. He was mourned by all the people as if each of them had lost a member of his or her own family.

You probably know that when a President dies the Vice-President takes his place. McKinley's Vice-President was a capable man named Theodore Roosevelt. He was very fond of tramping through the wilds and of hunting wild beasts. At the time we speak of, when the news of the death of President McKinley was sent abroad, Vice-President Roosevelt was off on a long tramp through the Adirondack Mountains of New York, perhaps hoping to shoot a deer, or possibly a bear.

When the news came, no one knew where he was, and dozens of the mountain-climbers were sent out to find him. As they spread out and pushed forward, the crack of rifles could be heard on all sides and megaphones were used to send their voices far through the mountain defiles. But hour after hour passed and the shades of evening were at hand, and still no answer came; no sign of Roosevelt and his party could be traced. Finally, when they were near the high top of Mount Marcy, answering shots and shouts were heard, and soon the hunting party came in sight.

When Mr. Roosevelt was told the news they brought—that the President was at the point of death—he could hardly believe it; for the last news had said that he was likely to get well. He knew now that he must get to Buffalo as soon as he could, so that the country should not be without a President, and he started back for the clubhouse from which he had set out at a pace that kept the others busy to keep up with him.

Night had fallen when he reached the clubhouse, but there was to be no sleep for him that night. A stagecoach, drawn by powerful horses, waited his coming, and in very few minutes he was inside it, the coachman had drawn his reins and cracked his whip, and away went the horses, plunging into the darkness of the woods that overhung the road.

That was one of the great rides in our history. You would have said so if you had been there to see. There were thirty-five miles to be made before the nearest railroad station could be reached. The road was rough and muddy, for a very heavy thunderstorm had fallen that day. Darkness overhung the way, made more gloomy by the thick foliage of the trees. Here and there they stopped for a few minutes to change horses, and then plunged on at full speed again. What thoughts were in the mind of the solitary passenger whom fate was about to make President of the great United States, during that dark and dismal night, no one can tell. Fortune had built for him a mighty career and he was hastening to take up the reins of government, soon to be dropped by the man chosen to hold them.

Alden's Lane was reached at 3:15 in the morningand the horses were again changed. The road now before them was the worst of all, for it was very narrow in places and had deep ravines on either side, while heavy forest timber shut it in. But the man who handled the horses knew his road and felt how great a duty had been placed in his hands, and at 5:22 that morning, when the light of dawn was showing in the east, the coach dashed up to the railroad station at North Creek. Here a special train, the locomotive puffing out steam, lay waiting for its distinguished passenger.

News of greater weight now greeted the traveler. He was told that the President was dead. He had passed away at Buffalo three hours before. The man who landed as Vice-President on that solitary platform, was now President of the United States. Only the oath of office was needed to make him such.

Disturbed in mind by the thrilling news, the traveler of the night stepped quickly into the car that waited for him, and the engine darted away through the dawn of the new day. Speed, speed, speed, was the thought in the mind of the engineer, and over the track dashed the iron horse and its single car, often at a rate of more than a mile a minute. Hour after hour passed by as they rushed across the state. At 1:40 in the afternoon the train came rattling into Buffalo, and its passenger leaped to the platform and made all hasteto the house of Ainsley Wilcox, one of his special friends. There, that afternoon, he was sworn into office as President of the United States, and the scene we have described came to an end, one of the most dramatic among those in our country's history. Never before had a man been sought in the depths of a mountain wilderness and ridden through rain and gloom a whole night long, to be told at the end that he had become the ruler of one of the greatest nations on the earth!

I have told you that Theodore Roosevelt was fond of hunting. While he was President he had to leave the wild animals alone, but he did another kind of hunting, which was to hunt for dishonesty and fraud among the great business concerns of the country. He said that every man ought to have an equal chance to make a living, and he had laws passed to help in this.

This kind of hunting made him very popular among the people, which was shown by his being elected President by a large majority when the time came for the next Presidential election. He also won much fame by helping to put an end to the dreadful war between Russia and Japan, and men everywhere began to speak of him as the greatest of living rulers.

While Mr. Roosevelt was President several things took place which are worth speaking about. One was the building of the Panama canal toconnect the Atlantic and Pacific oceans. It is not yet finished, but when it is done it will be the greatest canal on the earth. A second thing was the splendid World's Fair held at St. Louis in 1904, in memory of the purchase from France of the great Louisiana country a century before. Two years later the large city of San Francisco was destroyed by earthquake and fire, with great loss of life and property.

One thing more must be spoken of, for with this President Roosevelt had much to do. This was to have great dams built on the mountain streams of the West, so as to bring water to millions of acres of barren lands and make them rich and fertile. Also, to save the forests, nearly 200,000,000 acres of forest land were set aside as the property of the nation and kept from the axes of the woodcutters.

The time for another Presidential election came In 1908, but Mr. Roosevelt would not run for the office again. I fancy he was tired of it and wanted to do some real hunting, for he soon set out for Africa, the land of the largest and fiercest animals on the earth. Here is the elephant, the rhinoceros, the lion, the wild buffalo and other savage beasts, and he spent a year in killing these animals and in keeping them from killing him. I have no doubt you would like to read of the exciting time he had in this great hunting trip, but I must stop here and leave it untold, for it is no part of the Story of Our Country.

9 789362 923271